AMERICA'S GREAT PARKING SCAM

You've Been Robbed

Kerry Lutz

Firestarter Publishers,
Palm Beach County,
Florida 2026

AMERICA'S GREAT PARKING SCAM

You've Been Robbed

This publication is provided for informational, educational, and documentary purposes only. It does not constitute legal advice. The author is not acting as an attorney in connection with this work.

All factual assertions herein are based on publicly available records, direct observation, photographic evidence, and good-faith analysis. Opinions are clearly identified as such.

References to statutes, regulations, manuals, and standards (including the MUTCD) are cited for descriptive and informational purposes only.

Any resemblance to actual persons or entities is factual, coincidental, or arises from documented public conduct.

ISBNS:

Ebook: 978-1-970521-05-4

Hardback: 978-1-970521-06-1

Paperback: 978-1-970521-07-8

Printed in the United States of America.

First Edition

Notice and Record Statement

This publication is intended to preserve and present a documentary record of observed conditions, signage practices, regulatory frameworks, and enforcement mechanisms relating to on-street parking systems in the United States.

The materials herein are based on publicly accessible records, direct observation, photographic evidence, municipal documents, published standards, and good-faith analysis. Where interpretations are offered, they are presented as opinion and commentary, not as statements of law.

Nothing in this book is intended to encourage or facilitate the violation of any law, ordinance, or regulation. Readers are encouraged to comply with all applicable laws while remaining informed of the standards, procedures, and rights that govern public spaces and public enforcement systems.

This work is not offered as legal advice, nor does it create an attorney-client relationship. The author expressly disclaims any intent to provide individualized legal guidance. Readers seeking legal advice should consult qualified counsel in their jurisdiction.

This publication is further intended to serve as a notice of record regarding systemic practices discussed herein, including the use of signage, payment systems, and enforcement methods in public rights-of-way. The inclusion of any entity, practice, or example is for documentary and informational purposes only.

CONTENTS

Introduction

My name is Kerry Lutz. By training, I am a recovering attorney. By temperament, I am a systems analyst and algorithm decoder. For more than fifteen years as an author and podcaster, my work has focused on how complex systems actually function—not as they are described, but as they operate in practice. Where systems remain aligned with their stated purpose, they work. Where they drift, they fail —predictably, repeatedly, and at public expense.

I have spent my career studying legal, financial, and civic systems to understand where structure turns into dysfunction. Systems do not fail randomly. Confusion is not an accident. When rules become opaque, signals conflict, and enforcement accelerates faster than notice, the system has already departed from its legitimate role.

I am suspicious of all extractive structures—systems that take from the public without providing corresponding value. I abhor corruption, but more importantly, I reject institutional gaslighting: the insistence that confusion is compliance, that coercion is choice, and that revenue collection is regulation.

Those principles led me to closely examine what I now call the *Parking Industrial Complex*.

Parking regulation did not begin as a punishment regime. The first meters were introduced to fund safe, affordable off-street parking and to promote parking space turnover. Over time, municipalities discovered a different use: automated, low-resistance revenue extraction. That deviation hardened into policy. Policy hardened into dependency. And dependency hardened into a nationwide structure that increasingly bears little resemblance to legitimate regulation and proper intent.

Today, drivers face conflicting signage, hidden terms, digital payment traps, aggressive penalties, and procedural shortcuts that undermine basic principles of notice, due process, and fairness. Instead of clarity, there is confusion. Instead of fair warning, there is assumption. Instead of regulation, there is extraction. These are not isolated failures; they are intended systemic features.

This book analyzes and explains this disturbing trend—how it occurred, how it persists, and how it can be corrected. It is neither an attack on the government nor on the individuals who work within it. It is an argument that regulation exists to serve the public, not to entrap it. When that relationship reverses, correction is not optional; it is necessary.

Some will argue that reform carries financial consequences for municipalities that rely on this revenue. Those consequences are neither accidental nor unjust. A government that funds operations through noncompliant signage, punitive enforcement, and procedural ambiguity has already abandoned sound practice. Restoring alignment is not punishment; it is accountability.

Parking is not a trivial issue. It is simply the most visible one. Millions encounter it daily—often within steps of courthouses, city halls, and civic institutions meant to embody fairness and due process. What we learn by correcting this system applies far beyond parking itself.

I undertake this work with respect for the rule of law, for due process, and for the belief that properly aligned systems strengthen public trust. The question is not whether reform is possible. The question is whether we still have the discipline and integrity to insist on it.

Chapter 1

Revelation: We've Been Robbed!

I had been parking there for twelve years without incident. The same curb, the same routine, the same understanding shared by locals and businesses alike. Then one day, without warning, there was a ticket on my windshield, compliments of Riviera Beach. I observed no meters, no kiosks, no apps, and no informational signs announcing a regime change.

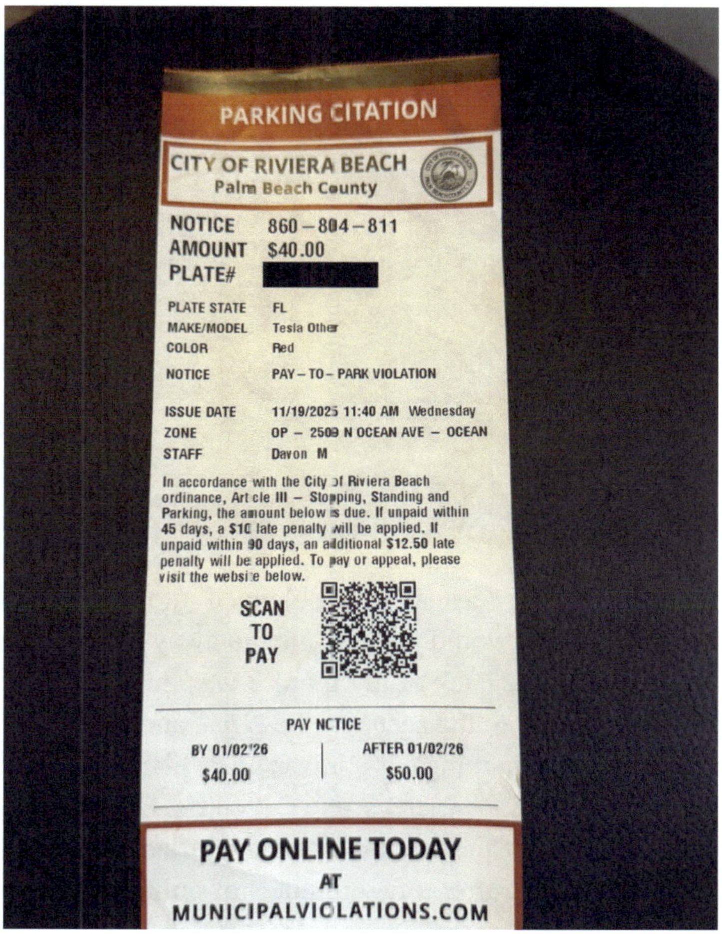

I never even noticed the sign because it just blended into the background. I took the ticket and left, figuring that I would just pay and go away like always. But something didn't sit well with me. In the back of my mind, I was thinking, where was the sign? How did I miss it? I returned to the scene of the *crime* and took this picture. The sign didn't look like a traditional parking sign; it was more like an advertisement extolling the virtues of Florida, beaches, palm trees, and QR codes. But wait, isn't there a federal standard for such signs? Isn't there a law against confusing deceptive signage? The answer was yes, there is, and after a few minutes of online searching, I found it, the Manual on Uniform Traffic Control Devices (MUTCD). Uncle Sam has his finger in everything, especially parking signage. And this sign completely failed to comply with any of the mandatory guidelines, from color, font, height, advertising, logos, and pretty much every standard created to protect the motoring public. Below are two examples of MUTCD-compliant signs. Notice the difference.

So then I did what millions of people should be doing all the time: I contested the ticket. The instructions did not send me to a courthouse, a clerk, or a hearing officer. Instead, they sent me to a difficult-to-locate web-based complaint-handling platform acting at the behest of the parking authority. There was no judge, no docket, and no courtroom —only a portal.

Within days, I received a response. Not from the court or the court clerk, but from a website known as MunicipalCitationProcessing.com. The ticket had been dismissed, not because I was right, not because the signage was improper, and not because there was no lawful notice. It was dismissed for "delay," though no one explained what delay had occurred or who was responsible for it. There was no court order and no ruling—just a digital message informing me that the system had chosen mercy. At first, I felt relief. Then I read the terms embedded in the communications. Those terms revealed what would have happened had the algorithm decided differently. If the ticket wasn't dismissed, I would have been forced to proceed under private terms I never agreed to. I was informed that we would be splitting adjudication fees and appointing a so-called neutral party to decide the case. I've been before dozens of neutral judges, and none ever ordered me to split costs. But then I never had a judge who came with terms of service.

Municipal Citation Processing

Hello Kerry Lutz,

This email is an acknowledgement of your request to dispute your charge 860-804-811. This charge has been put on hold pending a review.

In accordance with FL Statute HB271, a Charge issued in Florida may be disputed within 15 days of windshield placement or date mailed. Municipal Citation Processing may withdraw the Charge or respond within 5 business days. Within 10 days of receiving Municipal Citation Processing's response, you may appeal Municipal Citation Processing's response. If the Appeal is approved, the Charge is dismissed. If the Appeal is denied, you must pay the Charge. APPEALS WILL BE DETERMINED BY A NEUTRAL THIRD-PARTY ADJUDICATOR (EFFECTIVE ARBITRATION, INC.). PARTIES SHALL INITIALLY SPLIT THE FEE TO FILE AN APPEAL, WITH THE LOSING PARTY BEARING THE ADJUDICATOR'S COSTS.

Municipal Citation Processing

Hi Kerry Lutz,

We are in receipt of your dispute for non-compliance notice #860-804-811. We work diligently to provide dispute responses within an acceptable time frame. Because of a delay in our process, we are canceling notice #860-804-811 as a one-time courtesy. We apologize for the inconvenience. No further action is required on your part for this notice.

If you have already paid this notice, please note that we will be refunding your payment and no further action is required.

Thank you,

I didn't beat a ticket, but rather prevailed over a private digital adjudication pipeline. That was the moment it became clear that I had not violated a parking rule, rather I failed to scan a QR code. If I had used the app and paid the inflated fee, my stay would have been lawful, I think, (although I am not certain due to the ambiguous sign). Because I didn't scan, the same conduct became a violation.

In other words, the real offense was failure to submit to the parking masters: in the first degree. I searched the Florida Statutes for this offense, but it didn't exist. There is no law requiring citizens to download software to avoid punishment. Yet the penalty was real, enforced at the curb by an algorithm. The deeper I looked, the worse it became. Every layer revealed another defect, another missing piece of lawful authority. Instead of clarity, scrutiny produced confusion and contradiction. The more I looked, the more illegal it became.

Contrast this with a lawful system, where rights become clearer the closer you examine them. Here, law dissolved into software terms of service, and justice was rerouted through a URL. I had not beaten the system that day, but rather the algorithm had determined that I was more trouble than I was worth.

Not Just a Florida Problem—It's National

I live in Florida, and most of the examples in this book come from Florida cities. That is not because Florida is uniquely corrupt, careless, or incompetent. It's because Florida makes the problem easier to see.

Florida has adopted the Manual on Uniform Traffic Control Devices (MUTCD) verbatim. That matters. It means the rules governing parking signage, notice, and enforcement are explicit, standardized, and easy to verify. When a city in Florida replaces lawful on-street notice with apps, branded placards, meters, or QR codes, the violation is not subtle. It is visible. Documentable. Binary.

But the practices described in this book are not limited to Florida. They are occurring all over the United States. Across the country, cities large and small have quietly shifted away from standardized, on-street regulatory signs toward systems that rely on app-only payment and notice, vendor-branded signage, QR-code-based instructions, meters without accompanying regulatory signs, and rules buried inside apps, websites, or backend databases.

This shift did not happen because the law changed. It happened because enforcement became easier and revenue became more reliable when notice became ambiguous.

The MUTCD is not a Florida document. It is the national standard for traffic control devices. Federal law requires every state/territory/commonwealth/possession that receives federal highway funding to adopt the MUTCD or a substantially compliant equivalent. Local governments do not get to invent their own definitions of traffic control devices, nor do they get to substitute technology, branding, or convenience for lawful notice. Florida simply provides a clearer case study because it removes excuses.

In states where the MUTCD has been adopted verbatim, the analysis is straightforward: either the sign complies, or it doesn't. In states that rely on substantial compliance, the result is the same. Substantial compliance does not mean whatever the city prefers. It does not mean what the vendor sells. And it certainly does not mean that apps, meters, or QR codes can replace standardized regulatory signage.

Uniformity is the entire point of the MUTCD. Drivers should not need local knowledge, a smartphone, a data plan, or a proprietary app to determine whether parking is legal. The law must be visible at the curb, at the moment of decision, in a standardized form that looks like the law everywhere in the country.

What has changed is not the standard, but behavior. Cities have allowed parking enforcement to drift from a compliance-based system to a revenue-based one. Vendors design signs for marketing, not legality. Municipalities remove physical signs to reduce costs and clutter. Enforcement continues anyway. Most drivers pay without questioning. Appeals are quietly dismissed at high rates when challenged. The system works precisely because most people never challenge it.

Florida is not the exception. It is the canary. The same vendors operate nationwide. The same software platforms are deployed in hundreds of cities. The same design shortcuts appear in coastal towns, tourist districts, downtown cores, and college neighborhoods across the country. The same rationalizations are offered everywhere: "Everyone knows," "It's in the app," "There's an ordinance," "This is how modern parking works." None of those statements replaces lawful notice.

This book is not an attack on technology. Apps can be useful. Digital payment can be convenient. Modernization is not the problem. Substitution is. When cities substitute apps for signs, branding for standards, and convenience for legality, they are not modernizing parking enforcement. They are dismantling the framework that makes enforcement lawful.

Florida provides clear, photographable examples because the rules are explicit and the deviations are obvious. But if you live in California, New York, Texas, Illinois, Massachusetts, or almost anywhere else, and this feels familiar, that's not a coincidence. It's the same system. Different cities. Same shortcuts. Same incentives. Same result. Same extraction from your wallet.

What you are reading is not a Florida story. It's a national one.

The Scofflaw Doctor and the Trap of Patterns

My initiation into the true nature of parking systems didn't come from a courtroom, a statute, or a municipal code. It came from family. Back when my brother-in-law was attending medical school in Chicago, he lived on caffeine, exhaustion, and the naive belief that parking laws were merely "suggestions." Chicago, in its finite creativity, had other ideas.

Every day, he would speed into his rotations, park wherever he could wedge the car, and tear off for rounds. Five tickets a day wasn't unusual—sometimes more. They accumulated with the reliability of sunrise. By the end of the semester, his glove box looked like a municipal recycling bin dedicated exclusively to his offenses.

He didn't have contempt for the law so much as complete disregard for the system itself. He treated tickets like spam email. With New Jersey plates, he believed he was untouchable. And every three months, right on schedule, he'd legally swap those plates out like he was rotating disguises in the world's least subtle spy movie. This process went on for years, with abandoned license plates stacking up like unpaid tickets.

But there is one thing no one—especially a doctor on call—escapes: patterns. He parked in the same forbidden slices of asphalt every single day. He arrived at the same time. He left at the same time. His routine was a metronome, and the City of Chicago, which has monetized patterns since the dawn of graft, was simply waiting for the unpaid fines and penalties to reach a threshold where attention would be drawn, yet another pattern met.

My father—*Firestarter* Nat—saw this coming long before any policeman or tow truck driver did. Nat, having survived flying the ultra-dangerous *Hump* (the Himalayas between India and China) during World War II, understood systems better than anyone I've ever known. He could see a pattern forming the way a seasoned pilot sees weather before it appears on radar.

One day, he looked at my brother-in-law as he was receiving yet another packet of fresh license plates direct from the NJ DMV and said the line that became scripture in our family: "Vic, you do anything wrong long enough, and you're gonna get caught." Not a lecture. Not a sermon. Just a simple truth from a man who understood how systems behave and exact retribution.

While youth believes it's invincible, Chicago only believes in two things: enforcement and revenue. And one day, those two philosophies met. My brother-in-law walked out after a long shift, and the car wasn't there. Vanished. Gone. Evaporated from the streets of Chicago as if scooped up by some municipal rapture.

He marched to the local precinct with righteous indignation. "I'm Dr. Berger," he said. "My car has been stolen." The desk sergeant didn't blink. He simply said, "Wait here."

Moments later an officer appeared. "Dr. Berger, you're under arrest."

The system responded—not on day one, not on month ten, but years later, as it always inevitably did. Exactly as *Firestarter* Nat predicted. Vic eventually hired a connected attorney, a fixer—because this was/is Chicago—and escaped tens of thousands in fines by paying a few thousand in tribute. A civic discount available only in cities where corruption has been normalized and systematized.

But the real lesson wasn't in the money or the arrest. The lesson was this: People don't get trapped by laws—they get caught up by their own patterns. Systems don't respond to violations—they respond to repetition. My brother-in-law thought he was outsmarting the city. But the city wasn't studying him. It was recording his data and his habits. And that is the first truth everyone must understand in order to comprehend the Parking Industrial Complex: Parking enforcement isn't about order. It's about predictability. Predictability is the most exploitable resource in American corporate and municipal life.

And those parking apps can feel your patterns and predict your next move before you even know you're going to do it. The story stayed with me because my father saw the system long before the system sprang its trap. Army life taught him that if you don't understand the system you're living inside of, you will eventually become one of its data points, and you will pay dearly. And that's why this book exists.

The Reasonable Law-School Dropout Test

The system described in this book is not merely flawed or imperfect. It is corrupt, illegal, and unconstitutional, according to the allegations listed in my court complaint. Those conclusions do not require advanced legal theory, technical expertise, or years of courtroom experience.

In fact, the illegality is so obvious that even a reasonable law-school dropout would immediately recognize it as such. Clear notice is absent. Lawful conduct is punished. Courts are placed behind private portals. Payment is always presented before justice. Punitive revenues are optimized while due process is treated as an inconvenience or a mere afterthought.

That reality matters for one simple reason: if any reasonable law-school dropout can see that this system is corrupt, illegal, and unconstitutional, then how could the people who designed, approved, and deployed it not know what they were doing?

This was not an accident. It was not a misunderstanding. It was not a technical oversight. It was a design choice—one that relied on obscurity, intimidation, and the assumption that no one would ever slow down long enough to connect the dots.

This book exists to prove that assumption was wrong.

Chapter 2

From Allocation to Extraction: The Birth of the Parking Industrial Complex

According to a top traffic engineer I spoke with, parking did not begin as a scam. It began as a practical solution to a real urban problem: how to allocate scarce curb space in busy commercial areas. Early parking systems relied on time limits, modest fees, and mechanical meters to encourage turnover and prevent long-term vehicle storage. These tools were designed by traffic engineers, not revenue managers, and their success was measured by circulation, not collections. In that original model, parking fees served a legitimate regulatory function. They nudged behavior just enough to keep cars moving and spaces available while helping cover the modest costs of enforcement and infrastructure. Revenue existed, but it was incidental to the goal of turnover. The system worked because incentives were aligned around access and flow, not yield.

For decades, courts accepted this framework because fees were truly incidental to the goal. It regulated conduct, approximated cost, and served a narrow public purpose tied to traffic management. Merchants benefited from improved customer access, drivers benefited from space availability, and cities benefited from calmer streets. Parking earned its regulatory classification because it functioned as regulation.

Over time, however, the incentives began to shift. As downtowns redeveloped and municipal budgets tightened, parking revenue stopped being incidental and became an attractive funding source. What had once been a traffic tool gradually transitioned into a balance-sheet line item. Parking stopped being evaluated by turnover and began to be evaluated by yield.

That transition wasn't sudden. It occurred quietly, through incremental policy decisions that were rarely debated. Time limits were extended or eliminated, short-stay zones disappeared, and pricing replaced movement as the primary control mechanism. Enforcement priorities shifted away from overstays and toward nonpayment, subtly redefining what it meant to comply.

Technology accelerated the transformation. Smart meters, license-plate recognition, and mobile payment apps removed payment friction while dramatically increasing enforcement capacity. What once required judgment and discretion became automated, scalable, and data-driven. Parking could now be optimized rather than merely managed.

This was the moment allocation gave way to extraction. Parking apps did not instruct drivers to move along once a regulatory goal was met; they encouraged drivers to stay longer and keep paying. Session extensions were frictionless, warnings were designed to prevent lost revenue, and time limits became secondary to payment duration. The curb ceased to function as a shared civic resource and began to function as a monetized asset.

The advent of private vendors completed the transformation. Cities were told that outsourcing enforcement and payment systems was modernization and efficiency. In reality, it introduced a new incentive structure in which private companies were compensated based on transactions, collections, or volume. Revenue optimization was no longer an accidental byproduct of regulation; it became the business model itself.

At that point, the Parking Industrial Complex was perfected. Municipalities, vendors, enforcement contractors, consultants, and software providers became aligned around a single metric: dollars per space per hour. Turnover, access, and traffic calming receded into the background while yield maximization took center stage. The system rewarded extraction and quietly penalized restraint.

Despite this shift, the language surrounding parking never changed. Cities continued to describe parking charges as regulatory fees because that's what they had always been called. Courts continued to treat them as such because no one asked them to reconsider the classification in light of the new architecture. Drivers continued to pay because the amounts were small and the hassle of contesting was large.

Nighttime parking revealed the truth more clearly than any policy document. In entertainment districts, the pretense of turnover disappeared entirely. Cities wanted drivers to stay parked longer, spend more money nearby, and continue feeding the meter. Time limits vanished, rates increased, and the only meaningful violation became failure to pay.

At that point, parking no longer regulated movement at all. It monetized presence. The system stopped asking whether a space was being used efficiently and started asking whether it was producing the maximum possible revenue. That shift marked the final break from allocation to extraction.

Once parking operated this way, it ceased to function as a fee in any meaningful legal sense. It no longer approximated cost, no longer regulated behavior, and no longer served a narrow public purpose beyond revenue generation. It became a situational tax on access to city life, imposed administratively and collected one hour at a time.

The most striking aspect of this transformation is how little resistance it encountered. Parking lived in a legal blind spot created by low-dollar penalties, fragmented enforcement, and institutional habit. Courts saw individual tickets rather than integrated revenue systems, while municipal budgets quietly came to depend on the proceeds.

What emerged was not a conspiracy, but a combine—a self-reinforcing network of incentives that normalized extraction. Once parking became a dependable revenue stream, few cities could envisage ever living without it. Once vendors perfected monetization, no one wanted to return to allocation. Yet the law never changed. The legal framework that permitted allocative parking fees never authorized extractive parking taxes. The distinction was always there, waiting to be applied. The Parking Industrial Complex did not defeat the law. It grew in the space where no one was looking. And now that space, by virtue of this book, lawsuit, and regulatory complaints, has been illuminated for all to see. And the truth is ugly: billions extracted in bloated parking fees, excessive fines, booting, and towing. Not once was the public consulted by its representatives seeking input and comments about fairness. It became the *Doctrine of Pay and Go Away*.

The Mass Transit Justification—Accepted in Theory, Questionable in Practice

Cities often justify short-term parking zones and high curbside fees as a behavioral tool to encourage mass transit use. This theory has rationale and merit in dense urban cores with frequent, reliable, and accessible transit options. Pricing curb space can reduce congestion, increase turnover, and nudge commuters toward alternatives that better match urban capacity. Where transit is truly viable, parking policy can function as part of a coherent transportation strategy. Accepting that premise, however, requires examining whether the conditions that make it legitimate exist.

In most American cities, they do not. Transit systems are often infrequent, indirect, inaccessible to families, impractical for work schedules, or nonexistent outside limited corridors. Penalizing drivers in these environments does not encourage transit use—it simply imposes a cost on behavior that has no realistic alternative. High parking fees become punitive rather than corrective, transforming policy into revenue extraction disguised as planning. A behavioral incentive that cannot be acted upon is not an incentive at all.

Even where mass transit exists, the justification breaks down when parking revenue is diverted into general funds rather than reinvested in transportation infrastructure. If the goal were truly mode shift, parking revenue would be transparently earmarked for transit improvements, pedestrian access, or mobility alternatives. Instead, cities routinely rely on parking income to back-fill unrelated budget gaps. That financial dependence undermines the credibility of the policy rationale. A system that needs people to keep driving—and paying—to balance the books cannot honestly claim its purpose is to get them out of cars.

There is also a legal and fairness dimension that cities tend to ignore. Behavioral pricing does not eliminate the requirement for lawful notice, clear signage, and due process. Nor does it justify confusing, app-dependent enforcement that penalizes occasional visitors, workers, and service customers rather than habitual commuters. Transportation goals do not excuse defective execution. Policy intent cannot cure unlawful enforcement.

Finally, the mass transit argument fails when applied indiscriminately. Short-term zones and premium pricing may make sense in limited, high-demand areas during peak hours, but they do not justify blanket enforcement regimes, expanded paid hours, or revenue-driven escalation across entire downtowns. When pricing ceases to be targeted and proportional, it stops being policy and becomes taxation by another name. At that point, the stated goal no longer matches the system's real function.

The Demise of the Kiosk: From Friction to Forced Contracting

For years, cities preserved the appearance of optionality in parking payment. Drivers could feed a meter, walk to a kiosk, or download a mobile app. The app was presented as a convenience, not a condition of access. Officials described it as modernization rather than replacement. But the migration was always directional.

Meters disappeared first, justified as obsolete or costly. Kiosks were then reduced, relocated, or allowed to fall into disrepair. Screens failed, printers jammed, and "temporarily out of service" signs became common. Each inconvenience nudged drivers toward digital enrollment. The friction was not random — it was strategic.

On September 7, 2023, the Town of Palm Beach made the shift explicit. In key areas, parking became functionally app-only. Cash vanished, kiosks ceased to serve as viable alternatives, and the mobile platform became the gatekeeper to public space. What had been framed as preference hardened into structural design. The illusion of choice ended.

Other municipalities have followed the same path. Miami drastically limited kiosks in high-demand districts. Hollywood, Florida and Ocean City, Maryland embraced mobile-first models with minimal physical infrastructure. The national pattern is unmistakable: app expansion paired with kiosk contraction. This is not incremental innovation—it is systemic migration.

The kiosk was more than a payment device. It permitted a simple, one-time transaction without account creation. It did not require assent to evolving digital terms. It did not harvest location histories or profile behavioral patterns. It accepted payment and issued time.

Once the kiosk disappears, the transaction changes character entirely. To park on a public street, a citizen must now create an account with a third-party private corporation. That account requires agreement to the terms of service, arbitration provisions, data-sharing policies, and class action waivers. The driver is no longer merely paying for time; he is entering a binding digital contract.

Those contracts typically require consent to mandatory arbitration. They often include waivers of class participation. They authorize broad data collection, geolocation tracking, and behavioral analysis. Many permit unilateral modification of terms and cross-border data storage. None of this is optional once the kiosk is removed.

When access to public infrastructure is conditioned on acceptance of private contractual terms, consent becomes theoretical. The driver cannot meaningfully negotiate, refuse, or modify the agreement without forfeiting the ability to park. The transaction is adhesive in form and compulsory in effect. Public streets become gateways into private legal regimes.

When government access depends on private assent, the contract is no longer voluntary.

This transformation reframes the debate. The issue is no longer about convenience or modernization. It is whether municipalities may effectively outsource the right to use public space to a third-party digital intermediary. It is whether citizens can be required to waive procedural rights and accept arbitration simply to occupy a lawful parking space.

If the system is truly benign and efficiency-driven, transparency should pose no risk. Cities can disclose total app-generated revenue, vendor revenue splits, convenience fee retention, and data monetization arrangements. They can explain how much of the proceeds fund infrastructure versus general budgets. They can clarify whether parking flows support bonded obligations or securitized revenue streams. Sunlight either confirms legitimacy or exposes incentives.

It gets even worse. The imbalance does not end with data collection and arbitration clauses. Most parking app agreements grant the company unilateral authority to suspend or terminate an account at its discretion, presumably with or without cause. There is typically no meaningful notice requirement, no evidentiary standard, and no formal appeal mechanism. A citizen can be digitally locked out of the system without a hearing, explanation, or recourse. When parking is app-dependent, suspension becomes exclusion from public space without procedural protection.

The demise of the kiosk is therefore not administrative housekeeping. It is the moment friction gave way to mandate and convenience evolved into compelled contracting. Once the illusion of choice collapses, the legal character of the system changes. And once the legal character changes, scrutiny becomes unavoidable.

Chapter 3

THE MUTCD

The Law We Never Knew We Were Living Under

You see a STOP sign. You see a speed limit. You see a "No Turn on Red." You see a "2-Hour Parking/Tow Away Zone." You assume they are legal, accurate, and enforceable, and you obey them without a second thought. That assumption is not careless; it is the foundation of modern transportation and civil order. Society depends on drivers trusting that what they see on the road has legal meaning. Without that trust, the entire system collapses.

What almost no one realizes is that every one of those commands is governed by a single federal document that quietly controls daily life more directly than most laws people actually know by name. It governs how signs must look, where they must be placed, what they must say, and how they must be seen. Cities are legally required to follow it. Instead, many have ignored it for decades. That document is the Manual on Uniform Traffic Control Devices, known as the MUTCD.

The MUTCD was born out of chaos. In the early twentieth century, as automobiles spread across the country, traffic control was inconsistent and improvised from town to town. Signs varied in color, shape, size, placement, and meaning, even when they governed identical conduct. Drivers crossing municipal or state lines encountered unfamiliar symbols and conflicting instructions. Confusion, accidents, and liability predictably followed.

Engineers, insurers, and transportation officials recognized that traffic control could not function as a patchwork of local creativity. Drivers could not be expected to relearn the rules every few miles. What was needed was a single national system based on predictability, human perception, and uniform meaning. The MUTCD emerged from that recognition as an effort to standardize traffic control devices across the country. Over time, it was adopted by the federal government and incorporated into federal regulation.

Upon adoption, the MUTCD stopped being guidance, and it became law. It was adopted by every state as a condition to receive federal highway funds. Uniformity was no longer optional; it was mandatory. The MUTCD became the operating system of American roads, governing how the law speaks to drivers in real time. Whether people knew its name or not, they lived under it every day.

What makes the MUTCD unique is the depth of research behind it. Every requirement regarding color, contrast, font, size, reflectivity, height, placement, and wording was tested and debated over decades. Human-factors psychologists studied how quickly drivers perceive information at speed. Engineers analyzed reaction time, braking distance, and visibility under real-world conditions. The MUTCD assumes drivers are imperfect, distracted, and moving quickly, and it designs around those realities.

Just as important is what the MUTCD was never meant to be. It was not designed to be decorative, flexible, or selectively applied. Uniform is in its name because it's the core principle. Uniformity is what keeps drivers safe and informed. A sign that is hidden, confusing, improvised, or inconsistent undermines the entire system, not just that one location. Compliance is what makes traffic control fair, predictable, and lawful. And it is a potential hazard as some drivers slow down or even stop to read it. Accidents caused by such behavior happen daily.

Traffic law operates differently from almost every other area of law. You are not expected to memorize municipal ordinances before driving. You are not required to consult a website, download an app, or search for hidden rules. Traffic law operates through traffic control devices placed in the physical world. Those devices communicate binding legal rules instantly, without explanation or negotiation. The MUTCD rules specifically state that

A traffic control device is not just any sign. It is a sign, signal, or marking placed by lawful authority for the purpose of regulating, warning, or guiding traffic. That distinction matters because the device itself is the legal instrument. It is how abstract law becomes an enforceable obligation. Without a valid traffic control device, the rule has no lawful voice.

Notice is the foundation of due process. The government cannot punish a person unless it gives fair notice of the rule being enforced. That principle explains why lawsuits require service, why evictions require warning, and why secret laws are unconstitutional. You can only obey rules you can see and understand. On the road, the only lawful notice is a sign.

Apps do not provide legal notice. QR codes do not provide legal notice. Websites, parking meters, kiosks, portals, and "see app for details" disclaimers do not provide legal notice. Signs are the law in public space. Only a lawful traffic control device, a compliant sign, can speak for the government. Anything else is enforcement without notice.

When a city issues a parking citation, it is not enforcing an ordinance in the abstract. It is enforcing the command of a traffic control device at a specific location and moment in time. If an unlawful non-compliant device conveyed that command before the vehicle was parked, then no rule was communicated. Without notice, there can be no violation. Punishment without notice is punishment without due process.

Municipalities often try to blur this line by pointing to apps, kiosks, painted curbs, or generalized "parking zones." None of those are substitutes for a lawful traffic control device. The law does not permit governments to enforce invisible rules or outsource notice to technology. If a city wants to regulate parking, impose conditions, charge a price, or threaten penalties, it must do so through a compliant sign visible before the driver acts. If it fails to do that, enforcement is unlawful.

This brings us to the scandal. If your city charges for parking, the odds are overwhelming that its signage violates the MUTCD. Wrong colors, improper fonts, incorrect mounting height, insufficient reflectivity, contradictory time windows, missing arrows, hidden conditions, pastel palettes, or QR codes replacing instructions are the norm, not the exception. These are not technical nitpicks. Each defect undermines lawful notice. Throughout my travels through the state of Florida, I have only seen one sign that was close to compliance, but it missed several key points.

When required signage fails, notice fails with it. When notice fails, due process cannot be satisfied. Enforcement built on defective notice is legally void. And when enforcement fails at scale, the revenue model that depends on it collapses. Parking "revenue" in those circumstances is not income; it is a future liability.

Federal law has always contained a blunt enforcement mechanism for MUTCD compliance: money. States and municipalities receive federal highway funds only if their traffic control devices conform to the national standard. The MUTCD is the price of admission to federal transportation dollars. That condition has existed for decades.

Yet it has rarely been enforced at the municipal level. Cities learned that non-compliance carried little immediate risk. Signs could be improvised, apps could replace notice, and enforcement would continue anyway. Parking revenue grew while the federal hammer stayed on the wall. Not because it lacked force, but because no one forced a court to pick it up.

That changes the moment a federal judge aligns four propositions already embedded in law. The MUTCD is binding federal law. Traffic signs are legal notice. Non-compliant signs (or no signs at all like in West Palm Beach) cannot provide lawful notice. Enforcement without notice violates due process. None of these statements is radical on its own. Together, they are structurally devastating.

Once that sequence is acknowledged, the implications are immediate. Parking enforcement relying on non-compliant signage is unconstitutional. Citations issued without lawful notice are void. Revenue collected under those conditions is tainted. A city that continues enforcing parking rules through unlawful devices is not in technical violation of an engineering manual; it is defying federal law as adopted by its state.

This is why the issue has been avoided for so long. Enforcing the MUTCD does not tweak the system; it breaks it. The modern parking revenue model depends on the quiet assumption that notice can be improvised, delegated to apps, or ignored altogether. A single ruling affirming the MUTCD-notice-due process chain collapses that assumption overnight.

Some are of the opinion that cities did not abandon the MUTCD by accident. Clear signs reduce tickets. Visible rules reduce disputes. Compliant notice reduces appeals. So, signage was minimized, rules were hidden, and notice was outsourced to algorithms. The MUTCD was built for humans. The parking enforcement system was rebuilt for machines.

If the sign is unlawful, the enforcement is unlawful. If the enforcement is unlawful, the money collected is unlawful. If the money is unlawful, the system collapses. That is the American parking matrix. And once you understand it, you cannot unsee it.

No traffic control device. No notice. No ticket.

This Is Not an American Quirk—How the Rest of the World Handles Traffic Control

The idea that traffic signs must be uniform, standardized, and legally precise is not uniquely American. Every modern society that relies on motor vehicles has reached the same conclusion through experience, accidents, and litigation. The difference is not whether standards exist elsewhere, but how seriously they are treated and enforced. In that respect, the United States is not an outlier in theory, but it has increasingly become one in practice.

Across the European Union, traffic control is governed by harmonized standards derived from the Vienna Convention on Road Signs and Signals. Member states may retain minor national variations, but the core principles of uniformity, visibility, and advance notice are mandatory. A driver crossing from France into Germany or Spain is not expected to relearn the meaning of basic signs. The system is designed so that legal notice travels with the driver, not with the local bureaucracy.

European courts take signage seriously because signage is treated as law in physical form. If a restriction is not properly posted, it is generally unenforceable. Municipalities do not argue that a website, app, or mobile payment system substitutes for physical notice. The sign is the rule, and if the sign fails, enforcement fails with it.

The European approach also draws a clear line between regulation and revenue. Parking controls are justified primarily as traffic-management tools, not as municipal funding mechanisms. When cities overreach, courts intervene quickly because enforcement legitimacy depends on visible, comprehensible notice. The result is fewer tickets, fewer disputes, and far less public hostility toward parking enforcement as a concept.

Canada follows a remarkably similar model to the United States, but with a crucial difference in application. Canada has its own Manual of Uniform Traffic Control Devices, commonly referred to as the Canadian MUTCD. Like its American counterpart, it establishes standardized requirements for sign design, placement, visibility, and meaning. Provinces adopt it formally, and municipalities are expected to comply.

Where Canada diverges is in enforcement culture. Canadian courts are far less tolerant of municipalities improvising signage or substituting administrative convenience for lawful notice. If a sign does not meet prescribed standards, enforcement is routinely questioned and often dismissed. The assumption is that the burden of clarity rests with the government, not the driver.

Canadian municipalities therefore tend to err on the side of over-notification rather than under-notification. Physical signs remain central even where digital payment systems exist. Apps may facilitate payment, but they do not replace the sign as the legal voice of the rule. This preserves the basic due-process principle that drivers must be able to understand restrictions before they park.

Other developed nations follow similar paths. Japan, for example, enforces extraordinarily strict parking rules, but those rules are communicated through dense, unmistakable signage and pavement markings. Enforcement is severe, but it is also transparent. Drivers know exactly what is prohibited and why, leaving little room for ambiguity or entrapment.

Australia and New Zealand operate under national road-sign standards that emphasize consistency and advance notice. Courts there have repeatedly invalidated enforcement where signage was misleading, incomplete, or poorly placed. The concept that a driver should "check an app" to understand a legal restriction would be viewed skeptically at best. Physical notice remains paramount.

Even in countries with aggressive enforcement, the principle is the same: the rule must be visible before it is enforced. Governments abroad generally understand that traffic control works only if drivers trust what they see. That trust collapses when rules are hidden, mutable, or revealed only after punishment. As a result, signage compliance is treated as a prerequisite, not a technical afterthought.

What distinguishes the United States today is not the absence of standards, but the normalization of ignoring them. The MUTCD exists precisely to serve the same function as its European and Canadian counterparts. The problem is not that the American system is different; it is that municipalities have learned they can violate it without consequence. Apps, kiosks, and portals have been allowed to displace physical notice in ways that would not survive scrutiny elsewhere.

This comparison matters because it demolishes the argument that strict signage compliance is unrealistic or outdated. Other countries manage dense cities, complex curb regulations, and modern payment systems without abandoning physical notice. They modernize without erasing due process.

The United States could do the same tomorrow if it chose to enforce its own rules.

The MUTCD is not an antiquated relic. It is America's version of a universal language spoken on roads around the world. When cities treat it as optional, they are not innovating. They are regressing into a system where punishment precedes notice. And that is not modernization—it is institutional amnesia.

There isn't a single, universally agreed "winner," but among traffic engineers, courts, and human factors experts, there is a rough consensus hierarchy, depending on what you mean by *best*. The key distinction is breadth vs. rigor vs. enforcement.

How the Systems Stack Up

The United States MUTCD is arguably the most extensive single body of traffic-control law in the world. No other country has a document as long, granular, and exhaustively specified. It is encyclopedic. As part of this project, I purchased the 2009 and 2023 MUTCD editions. They are huge and cover virtually every possible traffic light and signage issue that has ever been encountered. The irony, of course, is that its strength is also its weakness: because it is so detailed, widespread noncompliance has become normalized.

Most Legally Respected and Enforced

The European Union system, built on the Vienna Convention and national implementing laws (Germany is often cited as the gold standard), likely wins. European courts consistently treat signage as *the law itself*, not as advisory. If notice is unclear or inconsistent, enforcement often fails quickly and quietly. The rules are slightly less granular than the MUTCD, but compliance is culturally and judicially enforced, which makes the system function better in practice.

Most Balanced and Realistic

Canada may be the most functional model overall. The Canadian MUTCD borrows heavily from the U.S. framework but is applied with far less tolerance for improvisation. Courts there are comfortable invalidating enforcement over defective signage, and municipalities tend to comply preemptively. Canada strikes a balance between technical rigor and institutional humility: the government bears the burden of clarity, not the driver.

Most Driver-Centric and Behaviorally Effective

Germany and Japan are often cited by human-factors researchers. Their systems prioritize immediate recognition, redundancy, and predictability. Enforcement is strict, but signage is unmistakable. The social contract is clear: rules are harsh, but they are never hidden.

There is very little tolerance for ambiguity, and almost no reliance on post-hoc explanations.

The Uncomfortable Truth

The United States has the best rule book on paper and arguably the worst compliance culture among developed nations. Other countries solved the problem by enforcing fewer rules very strictly. The U.S. wrote the perfect manual—then quietly stopped following it when revenue and automation became more attractive than clarity.

It all comes down to observance. The problem isn't that the MUTCD is outdated or unreasonable. It is regularly updated, and there are active committees at the Federal Highway Administration that are regularly reviewing the MUTCD and implementing improvements. The problem is that American municipalities learned they could ignore it, especially concerning parking, and still get paid.

Substantial Compliance: Their Only Out—and It's a Small One

Courts recognize the doctrine of substantial compliance for a practical reason: perfection is not required where the purpose of the rule has clearly been met. If a sign is mounted at 6 feet 11 inches instead of 7 feet, the law does not pretend the sign vanished. If a sign's retroreflectivity is slightly degraded but a citation is issued at high noon on a clear day, a court is not going to invalidate enforcement on a technicality. Substantial compliance exists to prevent gamesmanship, not to excuse failure.

But that doctrine has strict limits. Substantial compliance applies only when the essential purpose of the requirement—clear, advance notice—has been achieved. It does not apply where notice is missing, obscured, confusing, contradictory, or effectively invisible. A sign hidden behind foliage, angled away from traffic, mounted where a driver would not reasonably see it, unlit at night, or contradicted by meters or apps is not "almost compliant." It has failed its core function. That is not an inch off the mark; it is missing the target entirely. And if there's no signage at all, like in West Palm Beach, it's going to be interesting to see the result when it's challenged.

Just as important, substantial compliance does not mean municipalities may redesign legal notice into marketing collateral. Logos, branding elements, QR codes, pastel color palettes, palm trees, or decorative motifs do not advance the purpose of a traffic control device; they undermine it. A traffic sign is not an advertisement, a tourism brochure, or a design experiment. When aesthetics compete with contrast, legibility, uniformity, and instant comprehension, the sign ceases to function as legal notice. A sign that prioritizes branding over clarity is not substantially compliant—it is noncompliant by design.

Nor does substantial compliance excuse clutter or contradiction. Multiple signs stacked on the same post, conflicting instructions, fine print competing with pricing, or regulatory commands buried among unrelated information do not provide notice. Courts do not require drivers to solve a visual puzzle before parking. If a reasonable driver cannot determine the rule quickly and confidently *before* exiting the vehicle, notice has failed. Substantial compliance tolerates minor deviations where the message remains clear; it does not tolerate confusion engineered by excess.

Finally, substantial compliance cannot be invoked to justify novel substitutes for lawful traffic control devices. QR codes do not speak the law. Apps do not speak the law. Websites do not speak the law. The law speaks through standardized traffic control devices placed in the physical environment, visible before the act occurs. A city cannot claim substantial compliance by replacing required notice with "scan here," "download the app," or "look it up." That is not compliance—it is an admission that the sign itself is insufficient.

In short, substantial compliance forgives an inch. It does not forgive a redesign. It excuses a minor imperfection in execution; it does not excuse abandonment of the rule’s purpose. When noncompliance becomes widespread, decorative, technological, or revenue-driven, the doctrine offers no shelter. The law tolerates human error. It does not tolerate enforcement by ambush.

Chapter 4

A Brief History of the Parking Enforcement and Parking Control—The Accidental Billion-Dollar Monster

No one sat down one day and said, “Let’s create a system that quietly extracts billions from the public through confusing signs, predatory apps, and legal traps.” Like most bureaucratic disasters, the modern parking enforcement regime was a good idea when it was created, but it became layered with terrible incentives. What began as a tool for public order slowly mutated into a revenue engine—one so normalized that few people ever stop to question how it works, who it serves, or whether it still bears any resemblance to its original purpose.

1904—The First Parking Ticket

The first known parking ticket was issued in 1904 in Cleveland, Ohio. A horse-drawn carriage had been left unattended for too long and was deemed to be “obstructing commerce.” The logic was straightforward: streets existed to move goods and people, and anything that interfered with that flow needed to be controlled. There was no fine-tuning, no monetization strategy, and no notion of parking as a profit center. It was traffic and crowd control, plain and simple.

1932—The First Parking Meter

The first parking meter was invented by Carl C. Magee in response to a simple problem: downtown parking congestion. As automobile ownership surged in American cities during the 1920s and 1930s, employees parked all day on commercial streets, leaving few spaces for shoppers and hurting local businesses. Time limits existed, but enforcement by police chalking tires was inefficient and inconsistent.

Magee's solution was a small, mechanical, coin-operated device installed at each parking space. Drivers inserted a coin and wound the meter, which visibly counted down the allowed parking time. When the time expired, the meter clearly signaled a violation, making enforcement straightforward and objective.

The system worked. Parking turnover increased, downtown access improved, and cities gained a modest new revenue source to help fund street maintenance and traffic enforcement. First field-tested in Oklahoma City in 1935, parking meters quickly spread to cities across the United States and became a standard tool for managing limited urban parking. Magee had no idea he had just planted the seed of a future multi-billion-dollar extraction system.

1945—Post-War America: Rosie Becomes Rita

When World War II ended, America shifted abruptly from wartime industry to peacetime bureaucracy. Millions of women who had kept factories, shipyards, and offices running were suddenly surplus labor. During the war, the symbol of strength was Rosie the Riveter. After V-J Day, Rosie didn't disappear— she was repurposed. Cities needed civilian jobs. They needed order on newly congested streets. Car sales were booming, and the suburban sprawl was just getting underway. They needed enforcement. And women trained in discipline, logistics, and rules were the natural choice. Rosie the Riveter became *Lovely Rita*, the meter maid. Rita no longer riveted steel for bombers; she riveted tickets to windshields.

It was a cultural shift so subtle that almost no one noticed it, but it permanently altered the relationship between citizens and public space. Rosie helped win the war. Rita helped build the municipal revenue state.

Who is Lovely Rita? (For Readers Who Weren't Yet Born)

"Lovely Rita" is a song released in 1967 by **The Beatles** on their landmark album *Sgt. Pepper's Lonely Hearts Club Band.* The song playfully portrays a female meter maid—a relatively new and highly visible figure in postwar urban life—whose job was to issue parking tickets. At the time, meter maids were cultural shorthand: recognizable, mildly annoying, and symbolic of growing municipal attempts at order.

The song is lighthearted and flirtatious, but it captured a real social shift—the normalization of parking enforcement as part of everyday city life.

For readers born decades later, it's important to understand that *Lovely Rita* wasn't satire about corruption or revenue extraction. It reflected a moment when parking tickets were still seen as minor nuisances, not financial traps. Meter maids were human, streets were simpler, and enforcement felt personal rather than algorithmic. The song belongs to an era when parking control was visible, limited, and—crucially—understood.

That contrast is the point. *Lovely Rita* represents the moment before parking enforcement hardened into an automated, revenue-driven system. Before apps replaced signs. Before boots, tows, and escalating penalties. Before confusion became profitable. The Rita of the song was a person doing a civic job. The "Rita" of today is software.

Understanding that cultural reference helps explain how something once benign slowly evolved into the system this book exposes.

1960s–1970s—From Regulation to Punishment

As car ownership exploded and cities sprawled, parking enforcement hardened. What had once been a gentle nudge toward turnover became a system of penalties. Fines increased. Enforcement hours expanded. The idea quietly took hold that parking violations were not minor infractions but moral failures deserving punishment. The meter was no longer the message—the ticket was. Compliance gave way to deterrence, and deterrence gave way to income.

1980s-1990s Then came towing and booting—the moment parking enforcement crossed from inconvenience into coercion.

The Boot: From Enforcement Tool to Urban Infamy

The parking boot deserves special mention because it marked the moment parking enforcement crossed a psychological line. Unlike a ticket, which could be ignored or contested later, the boot was immediate, immobilizing, and humiliating. The most infamous version—the Denver Boot—was developed in the early 1950s by a Denver businessman named Frank Marugg. His invention was simple and brutal: clamp a heavy steel device onto a car's wheel so it could not be driven until the city was paid. No movement, no negotiation, no delay.

The *Denver* Boot quickly became a national symbol of municipal power. Cities loved it because it worked instantly and required minimal process. There was no need to chase violators, no need for court involvement, and no need to prove anything in advance. The boot reversed the traditional order of law enforcement: instead of *prove first, punish later*, it became *punish first, resolve later*. If you wanted your car back, you paid. Due process could wait.

Public reaction was immediate and intense. The boot was widely hated—not because people loved paying parking tickets, but because the punishment felt wildly disproportionate to the offense. Forgetting to feed a meter or misunderstanding a sign suddenly meant being stranded, late for work, or unable to pick up a child. In some cities, confrontations turned violent. Boot removals became a cottage industry. The device was vandalized, sawed off, torched, and even stolen. The boot wasn't just an enforcement tool—it became a symbol of government overreach and petty tyranny.

What made the boot especially dangerous was how easily it slid into revenue logic. Once immobilization became acceptable, escalation followed naturally: higher release fees, compounding penalties, and private contractors paid per boot applied. The goal quietly shifted from compliance to capture. By the time apps and automated enforcement arrived decades later, the psychological groundwork had already been laid. Citizens had been conditioned to accept that minor parking errors could justify immediate coercion.

The *Denver* Boot's infamy matters because it represents the turning point where parking enforcement stopped being about managing space and started being about exerting leverage. It normalized the idea that inconvenience could be weaponized, that mobility could be held hostage, and that payment—not fairness—was the fastest way out. Everything that came after—the tow truck, the algorithm, the app, the instant fine—follows the same logic the boot introduced. Once that line was crossed, there was no easy way back.

Not that towing was much better. It removed not just access to curb space but access to one's vehicle, often without meaningful notice or due process. Towing turned a parking mistake into a hostage situation. Travel to some godforsaken area of the city, find your car, pay all current and previous outstanding tickets, and you can have your car back. Out of money, out of luck. Initially, they didn't take credit cards. Cash was king. These tools were justified as necessary to control "repeat offenders," but they also introduced a powerful new revenue lever. Fees multiplied. Storage charges are accrued daily. Private contractors entered the picture, paid by the tow, not by fairness.

2000s—Improper Parking Becomes a Crime

By the early 2000s, improper parking was no longer treated as a minor civic misstep. It became a pipeline: citation, late fee, collections, license holds, registration blocks, even arrest warrants in some jurisdictions. What began as a nickel in a meter evolved into a cascading penalty system capable of ruining credit, employment, and freedom of movement. The offense never changed. The consequences did.

2010s–Present—The App Era and the Perfect Trap

Today's parking enforcement system is the logical endpoint of this evolution. Physical meters give way to apps. Clear signs give way to QR codes. Uniform rules give way to dynamic pricing. Enforcement is automated, outsourced, and disconnected from notice. The driver is expected to know invisible rules, changing rates, and hidden zones—on pain of fines, boots, or tow trucks. The system no longer regulates parking; it monetizes confusion.

What makes this monster accidental is that no single generation designed it. Each layer was added for convenience, efficiency, or budget relief. But together they formed something else entirely: a quiet, regressive tax enforced through threats rather than legislation, and justified as "management." The parking ticket was never meant to be a profit center. The meter was never meant to be a trap. Rita was never meant to become an algorithm. Yet here we are.

And once you see the lineage—crowd control to turnover, turnover to enforcement, enforcement to punishment, punishment to profit—you can't unsee it. The parking ticket didn't start as a scam. It became one.

The Parking Ticket Revenue Discovery and the Perfect Tax

The story of the parking app is the story of how big tech placed in the hands of revenue-starved municipalities, transformed a tool of convenience into an engine of extraction. It is the evolution of the humble parking meter into something far more efficient, invisible, lucrative, and satiable. For nearly a century, cities relied on metal posts with ticking dials to generate revenue. But beginning in the early 2010s, those posts began disappearing—not because the public demanded modernization, but because cities discovered a better way to monetize the curb.

The result is the modern parking app: a system designed not merely to collect payment, but to track behavior, automate enforcement, monetize confusion, and eliminate the physical evidence that once provided citizens with fair notice and legal defenses. This is the true history of the parking app, the philosophy underlying it, and the reason one "feature" will never appear: automatic renewal of expiring time. And it solved one of the great perceived *injustices* of municipal enforcement, leftover time on the meter. If a motorist paid for 2 hours of meter time and left prior to expiration, an opportunistic driver could claim that space and the remaining time. The app eliminated this *travesty*; cities could now get paid for more time than cars were actually parked for. They could now double bill for curb time: revenue took off. When lawyers double bill for their time, it's a disciplinary offense; when cities do the same, it's called revenue maximization.

The Pre-App Era: Pay Stations and The Almost End of the Standalone Metal Meter

Between 2005 and 2012, cities began transitioning from individual meters to centralized multi-space pay stations. These were large gray boxes where drivers purchased time and displayed a printed receipt on their dashboards.

Yet pay stations had their limitations: they still required physical presence and signage. They often malfunctioned and still produced paper evidence subject to challenge. The next step was obvious: limit or eliminate the hardware entirely.

Chapter 5

The Birth of the Parking App: The "Convenience Revolution"

Around 2012, companies such as ParkMobile, PayByPhone, Passport, and Flowbird launched pilot programs in tech-forward cities like Washington, D.C., Denver, Miami, and Seattle. The promise was irresistible: no need for coins or running back to the meter. Now you can instantly pay from your phone.

On its face, this was true progress. But the parking app was never really about convenience. It was all about data, automation, and achieving a level of revenue generation that physical meters could never match. Municipalities discovered that app-based parking zones delivered revenue increases of at least 20 to 40% in the first year. Not because people loved the app, but because the app made it easier to monetize mistakes.

The Golden Age of the Parking App

Between 2016 and 2022, the parking app industry completed its national takeover. What began as a convenience feature—*pay by phone instead of feeding a meter*—evolved into something far more powerful, profitable, and far more dangerous. Cities adopted parking apps for two reasons, convenience not being among them. Coins were inconvenient. The average motorist could only carry around so many quarters. How could a city charge $5 per hour, when a driver had to pay with change? That would require 20 quarters per hour or 80 quarters per four hours.

Credit card app-based parking eliminated coin-based limitations. Once cities transitioned away from coin-operated meters, they were no longer limited by the change in a driver's pocket. Their only became the driver's credit limit. This shift transformed parking from a coin-based mechanism into a high-velocity revenue extraction system.

But municipalities wanted more than digital payment; they wanted real-time usage data, showing exactly which blocks produced the most revenue, at what times, and under what conditions. They sought heat maps of compliance and noncompliance to enable the deployment of enforcement resources with precision. They wanted automated enforcement triggers—alerts that told officers where violations were statistically most likely at any given moment. And increasingly, they wanted integrated license plate recognition, eliminating the need for human judgment altogether. Enforcement could now be predictive rather than reactive.

This shift fundamentally changed the nature of parking control. The parking meter was no longer a neutral timekeeping device. It became the front-end interface of a software platform designed to maximize yield. Rates could be adjusted dynamically. Paid hours could be extended invisibly. Free periods could be eliminated without public friction. A single ordinance change could now be enforced across thousands of spaces instantly, with no physical infrastructure changes and minimal political cost. Parking was moved from Public Works to Financial Engineering.

Most importantly, apps delivered what cities had never fully achieved: predictable, bondable parking revenue streams. With digital payments, automated enforcement, and detailed historical data, parking revenue could now be forecast, securitized, and relied upon in long-term financial planning. The curb stopped being a place to temporarily store a vehicle and became a monetized municipal asset, optimized block by block, hour by hour to extract the maximum yield. Parking enforcement was no longer about regulating space; it was about managing cash flow.

Modernization was the justification. Apps were sold as efficient, green, and user-friendly. But modernization masked a deeper transformation. The driver's obligation was no longer defined by what could be seen on the street. It was defined by what the software knew and demanded. Rules became invisible. Prices became variable. Notice became conditional. Enforcement became automated. The law became subservient to code.

The net result was that the parking ecosystem had flipped. The meter had become software. The sign had become secondary. The human officer had become a node in a data pipeline. And the citizen had become a revenue event. The "Golden Age of the Parking App" was not about convenience—it was about control at scale, only made possible by technology and justified by the promise of efficiency. What cities gained in revenue certainty, the public lost in transparency, notice, and due process.

The Real Trap—Missing Auto-Renewal: Guaranteed

By now, millions of drivers have wondered the same thing: "If the app knows my time is expiring, and it knows when I go into violation, why doesn't it automatically renew my session or at least prompt me?" (Point of fairness to the apps, they do have a timer feature running and some do in fact send notifications that time is about to run out, however it requires you to have your phone nearby. And it's unhelpful if you are in a noisy place and didn't hear the beep or feel the vibration.

Technologically, auto-renewal is trivial. The app has your plate, your payment method, your mobile device, your location, and your parking history. It knows exactly when your paid period expires, and it knows when enforcement officers are nearby. It even knows, through geolocation data, whether you are still in the area. And yet, auto-renewal is absent. It could offer you the option to auto-renew for a set time period(s), and yet this omission is universal. This is not an accident. It is a deliberate revenue optimization choice.

Automatic renewal would dramatically reduce expired-meter citations—one of the most profitable categories of municipal income. Cities depend on revenue from violations to satisfy operating budgets, fund bond payments tied to parking income, and justify the enormous investments made in enforcement technology. If apps automatically renewed time, several things would happen: expired meter tickets would drop sharply, tow revenue would fall, enforcement officers would issue far fewer citations, and municipal budgets would face significant shortfalls.

In short, automatic renewal would remove the single most lucrative aspect of the parking enterprise: monetization of human error, which is why this feature will never appear. Because the system is no longer about turning over parking spaces, ensuring the public's ability to patronize local merchants. Now it's all about punitive revenue.

The Invisible Meter: When the App Becomes the System

The disappearance of physical parking meters does not mean parking rules have vanished. Quite the opposite. The rules have expanded, multiplied, and become harder to identify. What has vanished instead is visible legal notice. In many cities, and especially in West Palm Beach, traditional parking enforcement signs have been quietly removed or allowed to disappear. In their place, the city now treats the parking meter itself as the traffic control device—a role it was never designed to serve and cannot lawfully fulfill.

This inversion matters. A parking meter was historically a payment and timing mechanism, not a regulatory sign. It told drivers how much to pay, not *what the law was*. Time limits, enforcement hours, exemptions, and penalties were communicated through posted signs. In West Palm Beach, that structure has been flipped. The sign is gone. The meter remains. And the city now implicitly argues that the presence of a meter is sufficient notice that parking is regulated, paid, and enforceable—without clearly posting the actual rules governing that space.

At the same time, the modern parking app completes the erasure of notice. Cities argue that "the app itself constitutes notice," shifting the entire burden of discovering the law onto the driver. Rates can change by block, hour, or event without any new signage. Paid hours extend later into the night. Free periods quietly disappear. What used to be fixed and visible becomes variable and invisible. The curb is no longer governed by posted rules; it is governed by software.

The app-based system also removes physical evidence of compliance and noncompliance. There is no coin in a meter, no receipt on a dashboard, no mechanical proof that time was purchased. Everything exists only inside the enforcement platform and notices/texts. Officers receive real-time compliance data and automated alerts the instant a session expires—sometimes within seconds—turning parking into a precision-timed trap. Grace periods vanish. Human judgment disappears.

West Palm Beach's retention of physical meters does not solve this problem—it exposes it. Very few people feed quarters into meters anymore. Fewer still carry change. The city knows this. The meter remains not as a practical means of payment or notice, but as a stand-in for signage—a relic pressed into service as a legal shield. The meter is asked to do work it cannot do: communicate complex, shifting legal rules without actually saying them.

This is the core defect of the modern system. A traffic control device is supposed to speak the law clearly and in advance. A meter cannot do that. When signs disappear, and meters are repurposed as notice, enforcement does not merely become aggressive—it becomes lawless. The rules still exist, penalties are still imposed, and the revenue still flows. But the law is no longer visible. And an invisible law is no law at all.

Chapter 6

From Meter to Machine: Parking as a Data and Surveillance System

When parking enforcement migrated from physical meters to apps, the most important change had nothing to do with convenience or payment. It was the creation of continuous data streams. The parking app did not merely replace coins with credit cards; it transformed every parked vehicle into a data point, every driver into a tracked subject, and every curb space into a node in a behavioral monitoring network.

Modern parking apps collect far more than payment information. They capture precise geolocation data, including where a vehicle is parked, when it arrived, how long it stayed, and how often the same driver returns to the same locations. It also tracks account name, credit card charges, license plate, account number, and counts down the remaining time. Over time, a detailed behavioral profile is constructed: commuting habits, shopping patterns, work schedules, nightlife routines, even religious attendance or medical visits may be inferred from location history. This data is not incidental. It is the product.

Cities quickly realized that parking apps provided something physical meters never could: insight and revelation of human behavior at scale. Heat maps reveal where people linger and where they rush. Time-of-day analytics show when enforcement will be most profitable. Repeat-user data identifies "reliable payers" versus "high-risk violators." Parking enforcement stops being reactive and becomes predictive. It's eerily reminiscent of the movie *Minority Report's* Department of Pre-Crime as applied to parking. Officers are no longer patrolling streets; they are responding to algorithmic prompts telling them exactly where noncompliance is statistically most likely to occur. They've become the Department of Predictive Parking Violations.

Geolocation tracking is the backbone of this system. Even when anonymized on paper, location data is inherently identifying. Patterns do not lie. A phone parked every weekday near the same office building from 8:30 a.m. to 6:00 p.m. belongs to a worker. A phone that appears weekly at the same medical facility belongs to a patient. A phone that parks overnight in certain neighborhoods belongs to a resident. Parking apps know this, vendors know this, and cities know this. The data does not need to be "sold" to be valuable; it informs pricing, enforcement, zoning, and long-term planning decisions.

Behavioral data also reshapes compliance itself. Apps train drivers to internalize enforcement logic. Countdown timers, expiration alerts, and escalating warnings condition users to think in terms of *risk avoidance*, not civic cooperation. The moment a session expires, enforcement can trigger automatically. There is no grace, no discretion, and no human judgment—only a timestamp crossing a threshold, especially when cameras and license plate readers are in use. Parking becomes a behavioral experiment where drivers learn, through punishment, to comply with invisible rules dictated by software.

Crucially, this system flips the traditional burden of law. Instead of the government proving that notice was given and rules were clear, the driver is expected to prove awareness and compliance within a digital environment they do not control. If the app glitches, if GPS drifts, if a session fails to register, the data record still favors enforcement. The city's system becomes both the rule maker and the record keeper. There is no independent evidence left in the physical world.

West Palm Beach's decision to treat the physical meter as the traffic control device while stripping away enforcement signage makes this even more dangerous. The meter now acts as a visual decoy—a symbol of notice without substance—while the real law operates invisibly through data streams and software logic. The sign no longer speaks and informs; the app now does this. And the app does not speak to the public; it speaks to the enforcement backend.

This is the quiet transformation that defines the modern parking regime. What was once a visible, mechanical system governed by posted rules has become a black-box enforcement platform, powered by location data, behavioral analytics, and automated penalties. The curb is no longer regulated by law in the traditional sense; now it is governed by code.

And code does not explain itself. Code does not warn. Code does not forgive. Code records, predicts, and enforces. When parking enforcement crossed that line, it stopped being a matter of traffic management and became something else entirely: a low-level, ubiquitous surveillance system embedded into daily life, justified by convenience, and shielded from scrutiny by complexity and opacity.

All of which is why this moment matters so much. The issue is no longer whether parking is annoying or unfair. The issue is whether *law can be replaced by an algorithmic software system without notice, consent, or accountability*. Once the public accepts that shift at the curb, it becomes much easier to accept it everywhere else.

A personal Anecdote: Lutz vs. Pompano Beach, FL's Parking Combine

I learned how fragile—and one-sided—the parking app system can be in Pompano Beach, Florida. I parked, opened the app the same way I always did, and tried to pay. Payment rejected. No explanation. I tried a second credit card. Rejected. I tried a third. Same result. At that point, I had done everything the system supposedly required of me. The technology failed, not me.

So, I said *to hell with it* and went into a nearby restaurant. When I came back, there was a nice little present waiting for me on the windshield—a parking ticket. I was furious. I wrote the city a nasty letter explaining exactly what happened: multiple cards, multiple attempts, total system failure. I never heard back. No apology. No explanation. No acknowledgment that the app had malfunctioned. But something interesting happened next.

They never dunned me for the unpaid ticket. No follow-up notice. No collections letter. No escalation. Nothing. Silence. I eventually concluded that we had reached a kind of uneasy unspoken détente: I didn't pay the ticket, and they didn't pursue it. Call it even.

Later, I discovered this wasn't an isolated incident. Friends told me the same thing had happened to them in Pompano Beach—payments rejected, sessions failing, apps glitching. The difference was that they had paid the ticket anyway. Not because they thought it was fair, but because they knew how the system worked. Just pay and go away. That's the real rule. The ticket isn't about right or wrong; it's about friction. The city doesn't need to be correct. It just needs enough people to give up.

That anecdote captures the essence of modern parking enforcement. When the system fails, the risk doesn't fall on the city or the vendor. It falls entirely on the driver. The app is judge, jury, and executioner—and when it malfunctions, there is no meaningful appeal. The easiest path is always the same: pay the fine, swallow the injustice, and move on. That's not enforcement. That's extortion dressed up as convenience.

And this is why the parking app is the perfect machine. It doesn't need to work perfectly, just most of the time.

Chapter 7

How Your Parking Ticket Got Securitized by Wall Street and Is Paying for a 20-Something's Lamborghini

Most people think a parking ticket ends when you pay it; in reality, your ticket doesn't "end" anywhere. It begins a journey…through Wall Street's money machine, where your humble citation is chopped, sliced, pledged, securitized, sold, insured, re-sold, repackaged, and ultimately transformed into a bonus check for a 27-year-old named Hunter who drives a neon-green Lamborghini.

This is the Parking Industrial Complex. Your ticket and everyone else's become a cash flow, a bond payment, a securitized revenue stream. A financial product. The entire pipeline depends on illegal signage. If the signs are illegal, the parking fees charged are illegal, and the resulting ticket is illegal. If the fees and the ticket are illegal, the bond is worthless. And if the bond is worthless, the grift collapses.

Wall Street Loves Inflation (Why Your Parking Fees and Tickets Quietly Spike When Rates Rise)

Here's something Wall Streeters will never admit publicly: they love inflation. And not in an abstract economic-theory way. They love inflation because it's a windfall on every financial product they've tied to your daily life—including parking revenue bonds.

When interest rates rise, the cost of servicing those bonds rises too. And who makes up the difference? Not the banker. Not the app company. Not the city council. You. Because once a city securitizes its parking revenue, everything becomes backward: Bond payments go up, so parking costs must go up. Fines go up, and tow charges rise. Tow charges rise, and ticket volume mysteriously explodes.

All because the machine must be fed. A city can't tell Wall Street, "Sorry, we made our signs illegal for 20 years, and nobody's paying anymore." No, the covenants in those revenue bonds require revenue stability, growth, and sufficiency. It requires enforcement continuity, replacement of lost income, and "corrective action" if revenues fall.

And guess what "corrective action" means? You paying more. You getting ticketed more. You becoming the backstop for someone else's yield curve. The machine must be fed, and you are the main course on the menu.

Tobacco Litigation Bonds: How Wall Street Learned to Tax Behavior

Have you ever wondered why cigarette prices rose so much faster than inflation? The answer isn't health care, morality, or public safety. It's debt. Specifically, it's tobacco litigation bonds—one of the most revealing financial inventions of the last half-century. Once states realized they could securitize future tobacco litigation payments into bonds, smoking stopped being a public health issue and became a revenue stream Wall Street could price, trade, and depend on.

The Master Settlement Agreement didn't just punish tobacco companies; it monetized smokers. States received long-term payment streams tied directly to cigarette sales, and instead of waiting decades to collect them, many states (not including Florida) sold those future payments to investors upfront. That meant issuing bonds backed by future smoking. From that moment on, smoking cessation stopped being financially neutral. Every person who quit became a revenue shortfall that had to be made up somewhere else.

Here's the part nobody tells you: when fewer people smoke, the bonds don't disappear. The interest still accrues. The covenants still apply. The yield expectations don't change just because public policy worked. So, cigarette taxes rise, prices spike, and the remaining smokers—now fewer in number—are forced to carry a heavier financial load to keep the bond math working. The more successful anti-smoking campaigns become, the more expensive smoking must get to satisfy Wall Street.

This is the quiet genius—and moral hazard—of securitization. Once future behavior is pledged to investors, governments are no longer free to let that behavior decline naturally. They must *manage* it. Replace it. Penalize it. That's why cigarettes didn't just keep pace with inflation; they became inflation-proof revenue tools. And the cigarette producers tacked on their margin so their profits keep going higher. The cost isn't about discouraging smoking anymore—it's about servicing debt.

And this is where parking enters the story.

Municipal parking revenue bonds work the same way. Once a city securitizes parking fees, fines, and enforcement into a bond structure, parking stops being about traffic flow or turnover. It becomes a guaranteed cash stream. If interest rates rise, parking rates rise. If people park less, enforcement increases. If compliance improves, ticket prices go up. The system doesn't care whether signs were illegal, confusing, or non-compliant for decades. The bond requires revenue stability, and "corrective action" is built into the paperwork.

Wall Street loves inflation because inflation excuses price hikes without admitting motive. Parking fees rise. Tow charges jump. Fines quietly double. The justification is always vague—"costs," "maintenance," "technology upgrades"—but the real driver is debt service. Just like tobacco, once behavior is monetized, citizens stop being constituents and become yield support.

The tobacco bonds taught governments a dangerous lesson: you can securitize almost anything people do every day. Smoking. Parking. Driving. Existing in public space. And once you do, policy no longer serves the public—it serves the bond. The machine must be fed, and just as with cigarettes, if people try to do the right thing, the price doesn't go down; it goes up.

Hidden Illegal Parking Revenue Eventually Injures the Bond Market

The bond market is quietly exposed to parking enforcement risk in ways few municipalities acknowledge. Parking-backed bonds depend on uninterrupted enforcement, lawful notice, and stable public compliance. If courts determine that enforcement based on MUTCD-invalid signage is unlawful, the revenue streams backing those bonds can disappear overnight. That is not a policy debate—it is a structural risk.

Bond insurers, trustees, and auditors understand this vulnerability even if cities prefer not to discuss it. The uncomfortable truth is that many parking bonds only remain viable because the public has not yet challenged the legality of the underlying enforcement. Once citizens understand the law, compliance weakens, enforcement slows, and cash flow degrades. Illegal parking revenue does not stabilize the bond market—it quietly undermines it.

When parking revenue fails, cities do not merely lose income; they face refinancing stress, ratings pressure, and disclosure exposure. None of this occurs because of reform. It occurs because defective enforcement was normalized for years. Parking debt does not collapse from activism—it collapses from widespread illegality finally being recognized.

Chapter 8

Parking Apps Exploit Minors, Violate Their Rights, and Their Privacy

A quiet legal scandal lives inside the modern parking economy. It is not about signs. It is not about fines. It is not even about city budgets or predatory enforcement. It is something deeper, more structural, and far more troubling. Our Parking Industrial Complex is built on a simple but catastrophic flaw: minors cannot legally contract, yet parking apps and authorities treat them as if they can—and punish them when they can't comply.

In Florida and the United States, a sixteen-year-old can drive a two-ton vehicle on public roads but cannot obtain a credit card, cannot consent to financial terms, and cannot legally accept the contractual obligations embedded and hidden within parking apps. The law protects minors by restricting their capacity to contract. The parking industry ignores this, exploits them accordingly, and monetizes as if they were adults. And there are millions of them on our roads and highways, with more added every hour.

Most, if not all, parking apps require users to accept binding terms of service, late fees, arbitration clauses, autorenewals, and financial liability structures that only adults can legally acknowledge. Anyone who downloads an app and accepts the terms of service enters into a binding contract with the app company and continues entering into contracts every time they park and pay with the app (or kiosk or by phone). Here's the catch: teenagers are not adults. A contract signed by a minor is voidable—meaning the minor can walk away from the contract at any time, now or years into the future.

This is not obscure doctrine. It is the backbone of American contract law. And it exists to protect minors from being exploited by adults or companies, exactly what's happening here. Yet cities, private parking operators, and towing contractors rely on these voidable agreements to impose penalties, fees, boots, and tows upon minors who cannot legally agree to any of it. Modern parking systems do something even worse: they effectively deny minors the ability to park at all unless they enter a contract they are legally incapable of forming. Some might call this **coerced contracting with minors**, but to the Apps, the towns and cities, it's just another day at the office.

A sixteen-year-old has a lawful driver's license issued by the State of Florida. That license grants the ability to operate a motor vehicle—including the unavoidable act of parking it. Yet cities and private parking lots require minors to use an app to park or an app platform or to use a phone number written in the tiniest of text on an illegal sign. All of this creates a legal impossibility: the child must enter a contract, but the child cannot enter a contract. They can argue that the minor has a choice to park elsewhere or use a kiosk or pay cash (in the few parking areas where it's still accepted). But kiosks are just another form of interface. They capture data, such as plate numbers and credit card info, exact location, and that information, like any other they obtain, is fed into the data stream. So the parking kiosk isn't a safe harbor.

That contradiction alone would be enough to invalidate the system. But the constitutional implications go further. When a government denies a licensed driver the ability to park unless they accept a private contract, it engages in unconstitutional conditioning and coercion—forcing the surrender of one right to exercise another. This is not merely unfair. It is a due-process violation. Cities cannot design systems that require the impossible.

And yet that is exactly what happens every day in cities across America. Parking apps do not ask a user's age. They do not ask for parental consent. They do not offer a minor-protection mode. The system was built around the assumption that every driver is an adult. That assumption is blindly false, illegal, and constitutionally defective. A minor using a parking app is not just entering a contract. They are tapping through a corporate fiction designed to extract money from someone who cannot consent.

The exploitation becomes even clearer when penalties are imposed. A minor cannot owe late fees, service charges, administrative penalties, or convenience fees, because those obligations arise from a contract the minor cannot accept. The city cannot lawfully escalate those penalties. A towing contractor cannot lawfully seize a minor's vehicle based on a coerced voidable agreement. A booting contractor cannot lawfully immobilize a minor's vehicle under terms that never existed in the eyes of the law. Each one of those actions is built on a foundation of sand.

The private parking industry fares no better. Stadiums, airports, universities, hospitals, shopping centers, and corporate garages all use app-based systems that rely on minors entering contracts. If licensed minors could not use parking apps, enforcement would collapse in school zones, downtowns, beach towns, service corridors, and everywhere teenagers routinely drive and park. Revenue would drop. Compliance statistics would falter. Bond coverage ratios would wobble. The system depends on pretending children are adults.

But the scandal goes far deeper. Because parking apps do not only demand financial consent from minors—they also demand privacy waivers. They require minors to agree to pervasive data harvesting, GPS tracking, behavioral profiling, third-party data sharing, and arbitration clauses governing privacy breaches. A minor cannot waive privacy rights any more than they can waive financial protections.

Every parking app in America requires users to consent to extensive privacy terms. These include consent to geolocation tracking, payment-data retention, metadata collection, usage analytics, and sharing of information with private contractors and enforcement vendors. A sixteen-year-old lacks the legal capacity to waive any of these rights. Thus, every data point collected from a minor is unlawfully obtained.

The app captures the teenager's precise location. Not an approximation. Not a generalized area. The exact curb, street, lot, or garage where they are physically present, tied to a specific time and duration. It records when they arrive and when they leave. It logs how long they remain. This is not theoretical data. It is real-world movement data connected to a real person in a real place at a real time. The teenager is not choosing to use the app the way someone chooses to download a game or sign up for a social network. The choice presented is coercive and binary: use the app or be punished. Use the app or risk a ticket. Use the app or face towing, booting, escalating fines, or worse. That is not consent. That is compliance under duress.

It also does not matter whether the parking is public or private. The violation occurs at the app level. The moment a parking app captures a minor's location, vehicle identity, and movement history without lawful consent, the harm exists. If that data is shared, sold, breached, or accessed by a third party with bad intentions, the risk becomes immediate and physical.

What changes between public and private parking is not the harm, but the liability. On public streets and in municipal garages, the city is complicit. It mandates or endorses the app, benefits from the enforcement, receives data, and profits from the outcome. The city cannot claim distance from a system it requires the public to use.

In private garages and lots, the facility owner cannot hide behind the app either. If a private operator requires or induces minors to use a system that unlawfully collects and shares sensitive location data, that operator assumes exposure. The app may be the tool, but the property owner is the gatekeeper.

What makes this especially disturbing is not just that the data exists, but where it goes. Parking apps do not operate in isolation. Below is a list of all potential third parties that PayByPhone can share data with. It's shocking in its list of potential participants.

1. Payment & Financial Processors

Credit card networks (Visa, Mastercard, AMEX)

Bank payment processors (Stripe, Adyen, global acquirers)

Fraud and risk scoring services

Purpose: Process transactions and prevent fraud.

2. Hosting & Infrastructure Providers

Cloud providers (e.g., AWS, Azure, Google Cloud)

CDN providers

Database backup services

Purpose: Store and serve app data globally.

3. Analytics & Performance Tools

App analytics platforms (e.g., Firebase, Mixpanel)

Crash/usage monitoring tools

Session and performance tracking

Purpose: Improve app functionality and reliability.

4. Marketing & Messaging Platforms

Email campaign systems (e.g., Mailchimp)

SMS/text message gateways

Push notification services

Purpose: Send alerts, promotions, session reminders, and updates.

5. Parking Operators & Enforcement Systems

Municipal parking systems (cities & parking authorities)

Enforcement partners using PayByPhone session data

Purpose: Provide enforcement access to paid session status (acknowledging local enforcement systems can read PayByPhone data when integrated).

6. Support & Customer Service Vendors

Call center software/services

Support ticket platforms

Purpose: Assist users and troubleshoot.

7. Legal & Compliance Recipients

Law enforcement (if required by subpoena or legal process)

Regulators (in investigations)

Courts or legal claim respondents

8. Strategic Technology Partners

Integrated mobility partners (e.g., SKIDATA for gated access) as part of product integrations or partnerships

Each link in the chain increases exposure. Each handoff multiplies risk. This is not speculative harm. It is structural danger. A system that knows where children park, when they arrive, how long they stay, what vehicle they use, and how often they return is not benign. When that data is retained, aggregated, or monetized, it becomes surveillance tied to punishment.

This is not just unlawful. It is potentially actionable under multiple state and federal privacy statutes.

While COPPA Children's Online Privacy Protection formally applies to children under thirteen, state privacy laws—including those in California, Virginia, Colorado, Utah, Connecticut, and Florida— extend heightened privacy protections to individuals under sixteen or eighteen. Parking apps have no mechanisms to distinguish minors from adults. They simply harvest everything, making every bit of this data tainted and of questionable legality.

And the constitutional problem returns with even more force. Forcing a sixteen-year-old to surrender privacy protections to avoid a parking ticket is unconstitutional coercion. You cannot deny a citizen the ability to comply with a law unless they first surrender rights they cannot legally relinquish. That is the very definition of a due-process violation.

Minors cannot waive privacy rights. They cannot consent to data harvesting. They cannot agree to arbitration for privacy claims. They cannot authorize third-party data transfers. Yet cities and private vendors force them into systems that require all those things. This is exploitation in the purest legal sense.

When a parking app collects data from a minor without consent, it commits a privacy violation. When it uses that data to issue penalties, boots, or tows, it compounds the violation. When it shares that data with third parties, vendors, or collection agencies, it escalates the violation. When it requires minors to waive all claims in arbitration, it enters the territory of unconscionability. No parent would knowingly permit this. However, none were ever asked.

Companies that would face massive public backlash for collecting children's data in any other context operate freely under the camouflage of municipal enforcement. Yet the principle is identical: children's data is being harvested, monetized, transferred, and weaponized against them—without legal consent.

Cities will not want this argument in open court. Parking vendors will desperately try to avoid discovery. The moment a federal judge recognizes that minors cannot waive privacy rights, the entire enforcement architecture collapses. The parking industry will insist this is incidental. That the data is necessary. That it is anonymized. That it is secure. Those defenses miss the point. The issue is not whether the system intends harm. The issue is that the system is designed in a way that cannot function without ignoring fundamental legal and ethical boundaries.

This chapter is not an accusation against individual attendants, city employees, or developers. It is an indictment of a structure that treats licensed minors as acceptable collateral in a revenue machine. A machine that securitizes compliance, monetizes enforcement, and quietly absorbs data it has no right to collect.

We are told this is modernity. That this is efficiency. That this is progress. It is none of those things. It is the normalization of surveillance imposed on children for the sake of predictable cash flow. And once that becomes acceptable in parking, it becomes acceptable everywhere else, too.

For decades, the Parking Industrial Complex—the Combine has relied on two assumptions: that no one would notice these issues, and that minors were insignificant outliers in the system. Both assumptions are wrong. Minors represent a large and legally protected class. Their rights cannot be waived. Their data cannot be exploited. And their constitutional protections cannot continue to be ignored.

As this truth enters public consciousness—and the courts—the Combine will be forced into a reckoning. It will discover, perhaps for the first time, that no industry built on the exploitation of legal incapacity and involuntary data harvesting can survive the light of day.

Chapter 9

Florida's Data Bill of Rights—And the Quiet Violations Embedded in Parking Apps

Florida enacted the Florida Digital Bill of Rights, codified at Fla. Stat. §§ 501.701–501.709, in recognition of a simple reality: modern digital platforms no longer merely process transactions. They collect, analyze, and monetize behavioral data at scale, often without meaningful user understanding or consent. The statute imposes affirmative duties of data minimization, purpose limitation, and

heightened protection for sensitive personal data, particularly where minors are concerned (§ 501.702; § 501.705). These protections are structural, not aspirational. Municipal parking applications now operate squarely within the class of data-driven systems the Legislature intended to regulate.

Parking apps are routinely marketed as convenience tools, but in practice, they function as continuous data-collection platforms. To complete a basic parking payment, users are required to disclose precise geolocation data, time-stamped usage history, device identifiers, and behavioral interaction data. Florida law permits collection only to the extent reasonably necessary to provide the requested service (§ 501.702(2)(a)). A meter does not require behavioral analytics, and payment does not require persistent location tracking. Data collected beyond that scope raises immediate compliance concerns under the statute's data-minimization mandate.

Florida law treats precise geolocation data as sensitive personal data because of its uniquely invasive character (§ 501.702(1)). When such data is collected repeatedly and combined with usage patterns— such as identifying repeat parkers, compliance histories, or duration tendencies—it becomes behavioral profiling in substance, regardless of how it is labeled. The statute imposes heightened obligations when sensitive data is processed, including restrictions on secondary use and enhanced consent requirements (§ 501.705(1)). Parking apps routinely normalize this level of data collection without providing meaningful disclosures or choice.

The statutory concerns intensify when minors are involved. Florida's Digital Bill of Rights explicitly recognizes that minors cannot lawfully waive privacy protections through generic consent mechanisms (§ 501.705(2)). Teen drivers, student drivers, and minors using family vehicles routinely interact with parking apps, yet those apps typically lack age-verification protocols or parental consent frameworks. Instead, they rely on boilerplate click-through agreements that purport to authorize the collection and use of sensitive geolocation data. Florida law does not permit implied or constructive consent by minors for such practices.

These risks are not hypothetical. In the early 2020s, a major parking-app provider, **ParkMobile**, suffered a data breach affecting approximately 21 million user records, including personal and device-level information. That incident ultimately resulted in a $32.1 million class-action settlement, confirming both the scale of data aggregation involved and the real-world consequences when such systems fail. The breach demonstrated that parking apps are not low-risk utilities; they are high-value data repositories. Nothing about their current architecture prevents similar incidents from recurring— whether at ParkMobile or at any other parking-app provider operating under comparable models.

Equally problematic is the routine sharing of collected data with third parties. Parking app privacy policies commonly authorize disclosure to analytics providers, service contractors, enforcement partners, and undefined affiliates. Florida law does not allow a covered entity to evade responsibility for downstream misuse once data is transferred (§ 501.702(3)). Re-identification, geotargeting, and secondary profiling—especially of minors—are foreseeable risks that trigger statutory accountability. Responsibility follows the data, not the disclaimer.

And who knows what protections these unknown third parties take, if any, to protect this potentially sensitive data. Everyday there are headlines of new data breaches and sensitive user information finding a home on the dark web. Many of these third parties may have already encountered such breaches, but their duty to disclose is uncertain.

Claims of user consent do not cure these defects. Under Florida law, consent must be informed, specific, and freely given, particularly where sensitive data or minors are concerned (§ 501.705). A driver seeking to comply with a municipal parking requirement is not engaging in a voluntary data transaction. Conditioning access to basic civic infrastructure on the surrender of statutory privacy protections undermines both the letter and the purpose of the law. Convenience is not a statutory exemption.

We cannot emphasize enough that there really is no choice but to use the App. Imagine getting out of your vehicle in a monsoon and waiting in line at a kiosk to insert your coins (if it takes them at all). Or in some cities, the nearest kiosk is a football field away. Or in Palm Beach (home of our current president), they are intentionally scarce to encourage you to use the App.

What emerges is a familiar pattern. A system justified as administrative efficiency expands into surveillance and behavioral monetization with minimal transparency and limited accountability. Florida's Digital Bill of Rights was enacted to arrest precisely this kind of drift before it becomes normalized. Parking enforcement does not require behavioral intelligence, and lawful compliance should not require digital surrender. Restoring alignment here is not optional—it is mandated by Florida law and those of other states as well.

This is not a Florida-only problem; just like non-compliant MUTCD signs, it is national in scope and effect!

Chapter 10

From "Just Pay the Ticket" to the Dunleavy Doctrine

There is an old legal parable every lawyer knows. A man receives a small ticket—ten dollars. It is wrong, outrageous, a matter of principle. His lawyer tells him, calmly, to just pay the ticket. The man refuses. He goes to court and loses. Now it costs one hundred dollars. He appeals and loses again. Now it costs one thousand. Still outraged, he takes it all the way to the state supreme court, where he loses once more. The final bill is ten thousand dollars. Furious, he storms into his lawyer's office demanding to know how this could have happened. The lawyer replies, 'I told you to pay the ticket.'

For decades, that story served as a warning: principle is expensive, and the rational choice is compliance. But that parable depended on one critical assumption—that the system, however frustrating, still provided due process. There was a court. There was a judge. There was a human decision-maker. The cost of fighting was high, but the process itself was real.

That world no longer exists.

Modern parking enforcement is no longer adjudicated by courts. It is administered by apps, portals, and algorithms designed for efficiency and maximum revenue extraction. Tickets are issued automatically. Appeals are routed through software. Outcomes are delivered without hearings, without judges, and without records that resemble judicial process. At least Kafka got a trial. Today, all citizens get is an adjudication portal and are told it's justice.

This shift renders the old advice—'just pay the ticket'—obsolete. What once reflected prudence now reflects surrender. The *Dunleavy Doctrine* holds that when a system of minor enforcement replaces lawful process with automated punishment, the rational response is not individual compliance but systemic challenge. The doctrine does not seek to collapse institutions. It tests whether they are capable of lawful reform.

Unlike the Cloward–Piven strategy, which intentionally overwhelms systems to force collapse, the Dunleavy Doctrine begins with a presumption of reformability. It asks a simple question: Can this system operate lawfully when forced into the light? If the answer is yes, it should be fixed. If the answer is no, it should be replaced. Any collapse that follows is self-inflicted and completely deserved and brought on by the parties feeding off of it.

The Dunleavy Doctrine and the Man Who Stopped Exxon

Every era of American resistance produces a doctrine—a framework through which ordinary citizens reclaim control from institutions that have forgotten who they serve. In 2026, from the crumbling landscape of illegal parking signs, predatory fines, and bureaucratic arrogance, one doctrine has emerged with enough force to change the system: The Dunleavy Doctrine.

It didn't come from Washington, Silicon Valley, or a prestigious law school. It was created by Charles P. Dunleavy, the original asymmetric legal warrior—a man who decades earlier proved that one citizen can stop a corporate empire dead in its tracks, for a while anyway.

I simply adapted it to today's modern algorithm-run world and put a few of my customary flourishes upon it. Together, we created a doctrine that blends legal precision, Sun Tzu strategy, satire, and systems-level rebellion. A doctrine designed not just to win cases—but to expose corruption at scale and give citizens back the leverage they lost.

The Doctrine in One Line

"When the government abandons clarity and fairness, citizens have the right—and duty—to use expressive legal filings to expose, disrupt, and dismantle abusive systems."

It is lawful.

It is peaceful.

It is devastating.

And it stands on the shoulders of the man who pioneered asymmetric legal warfare before the term even existed.

Charles P. Dunleavy.

Not an attorney.

Not a bureaucrat.

Not a man of wealth.

Some might say he was unhinged, living in a run-down rent-controlled apartment on Manhattan's West Side. His weapon of choice was a Remington manual typewriter, complete with broken keys, a copy of every municipal and court code book, and a refusal to be intimidated by anyone or anything.

From that tiny apartment, a unit worth less than the carpet scraps in Exxon's executive boardroom, Dunleavy launched the most unlikely siege in American corporate history. And for a while, he won.

The Siege Of 1251 Avenue of The Americas

In the late 1960s, when Exxon (formerly known as Standard Oil Company and at the time the largest company on earth) attempted to erect its towering global headquarters at 1251 Sixth Avenue, it approached the project the way mega corporations always do: with the assumption that everyone would step aside or fall into line.

Everyone did, except for the man paying $38 a month for a rent-controlled 4th-floor walk-up apartment. Dunleavy understood something Exxon did not: "Construction may be physical, but permission is procedural. And procedure is where giants fall." Unbeknownst to the higher-ups at Exxon, there was no legal method to evict a rent-controlled tenant who was current on rent and compliant with residency requirements. And much to their chagrin, not everyone could be bought off. And Dunleavy pressed every pressure point available. At one point, he had multiple conflicting actions in the New York State Supreme Court, the United States District Court for the Southern District of New York, along with numerous complaints to various city agencies regarding environmental filings, notice requirements, affidavit defects, and everything in between.

He even wrote a vanity book, which my family's legal printing company typeset for him, *Up the Rockefellers*. It was several hundred dense, incoherent pages that no one actually read, but that didn't seem to matter to Dunleavy.

Eventually, he sued our company along with a federal judge for $28 million dollars, alleging collusion between our company and the judge. We were fortunate as the US Attorney defended us, and the case was quickly and quietly disposed of.

And with those tools, this single tenant halted Exxon's multi-million-dollar project for over 6 months. Not with money. Not with politics. But with process, the very thing corporations and bureaucracies fear the most when wielded by someone they cannot control. And he cost them dearly, $250,000 per week in the late 1960s. Dunleavy claimed he was offered $2 million, an exorbitant sum in that day and he gleefully refused it.

But finally, when the courts failed, Exxon allegedly indirectly hired others to solve its problem through extraordinary means. It was rumored that a *tenant removal specialist group* was brought in and that they employed various questionable acts to hasten his exit. First, the building's sewer connection was disconnected, next the water, then electric and gas. But Dunleavy held on as if his life depended on it, and maybe it did. Finally, one cold winter night, again according to legend, several thousand rats were released on his doorstep. He suffered a rat bite and rushed off to the hospital. During his brief stay at the ER, something unexpected happened. Taking a page out of *Power Broker* Robert Moses's playbook, the building was demolished in the dead of night.

But Dunleavy wasn't finished yet. The New York Telephone Company (later to be known as Verizon) was attempting to build a new switching station in New York City's Chinatown. This required the use of eminent domain; the phone system is obviously a public necessity. Somehow, the tenants got wind of Dunleavy's accomplishments in slowing down Exxon, and he was enlisted to ensure a similar outcome. He wrote another book, Up *the New York Telephone Company*. Eventually, that building went up, but I would venture to say the displaced tenants got a much higher price due to Dunleavy's ceaseless search for justice and a reputation that surely preceded him.

However, Dunleavy's lasting contribution was not to be found at 1251 Avenue of the Americas or Chinatown, but rather in the Southern District of New York Courthouse. While his incoherent filings were executed with relentless precision, his inexorable presence exposed a fundamental weakness in the federal legal system: The courts were structured for deference to outwardly sane attorneys and litigants, not defiance by unhinged pro se's. His asymmetric warfare overloaded the system—not maliciously, but by insisting that the system itself follow its own rules, even if he never understood them himself. He would routinely shut down the clerk's office for hours and send long tenured clerks into the embrace of their pensions.

The Southern District could not ignore him, because this was the 1960's after all and people's rights had rights. So instead, they adapted to him. They created a dedicated Pro Se Clerk's Office, positioned at the very entrance of the courthouse—a unit designed to channel the filings of citizens like Dunleavy so the court could continue functioning. All filings by appointment only, please. An entire administrative apparatus was born in reaction to one man living in a $38 walk-up. That is the definition of asymmetric power.

Dunleavy proved that power is not about position; it is about persistence and process. Authority collapses when forced to follow its own rules, and one determined citizen, for a while, can check the largest corporation in the world.

While he didn't overthrow the system, he revealed it. He didn't rage. He complied -- harder than the system did. He showed the weakness in the machinery long before the parking-industrial complex revealed its own.

I Am the Architect Who Turned Dunleavy into Doctrine

Where Dunleavy demonstrated asymmetric legal warfare with no reasonable goal in mind, I operationalized it by always staying focused and keeping purpose within grasp.

My intention was to fuse Dunleavy's spirit with Sun Tzu's timeless strategy: "If your enemy is violating his own rules, you have already won." With that, the *Dunleavy Doctrine* became more than a story. It became a weapon. It became a lawsuit that doubles as a nationwide education system, an exhibit that becomes a viral meme, a QR code that's a red pill for America, and a legal action that shifts public consciousness. The *Dunleavy Doctrine* teaches us how to fight back—with clarity, courage, and satire, while always maintaining our sense of humor.

America doesn't decline because of villains. It declines because of unchallenged nonsense. The doctrine reverses this decline by empowering citizens to expose incoherent systems, challenge predatory bureaucracies, and weaponize process against abuse. This doctrine uses filings to educate the nation, humor to reveal truth, and to attack corruption at its most fragile point: legitimacy.

This is asymmetric warfare brought into the modern era—scalable, legal, humorous, and unstoppable. Parking is only the first battlefield. Once people learn how the scam works there, they begin to see the pattern everywhere.

Dedication

This doctrine, this book, this movement, and the upcoming Netflix series to come are dedicated to Charles P. Dunleavy—*The Original Asymmetric Legal Warrior, The Last Holdout, The Man Who May Not Have Stopped Exxon*, but temporarily froze them dead in their tracks.

Charles P. Dunleavy, you were the first to show that the citizen is not powerless. You were the first to prove that knowledge defeats size. You were the spark. Now the doctrine carries your flame forward.

Chapter 11

The Mirage of Municipal Parking Revenue

Why Parking Revenue Is an Illusion Unless It Actually Builds and Maintains Off-Street Parking

Cities love to claim that parking revenue is essential. They present it as a stabilizing force in municipal finance—a dependable stream of money that helps pave roads, fund schools, protect police budgets, and "pay for itself." But here's the truth: Parking revenue is not real revenue unless it is reinvested directly into the parking ecosystem—specifically, off-street facilities and their long-term maintenance.

Everywhere else, it is a mirage, a brief glimmer of cash that evaporates the moment you touch it. Municipalities pretend they're making money from parking when in reality, they're cannibalizing their own economic base, degrading infrastructure, and distorting public policy.

Parking revenue exists for one historically recognized purpose: To fund the creation and preservation of off-street parking capacity. Period. Full stop.

Once cities realized they could siphon parking dollars into the general fund, the purpose of parking policy changed overnight. Instead of managing traffic flow and funding infrastructure, parking became a means of extracting revenue from unsuspecting motorists.

Parking revenue became a shadow tax, an ATM for bureaucrats, and a bond repayment machine.

And once parking money filled the general fund, the incentive to maintain actual off-street facilities collapsed. Garages decayed. Lots crumbled. Lighting failed. Concrete spalled. Security became a rumor. ADA compliance turned optional. Cities quietly abandoned the very infrastructure they claimed parking revenue paid for.

Suddenly, the city has a million-dollar problem it ignored for 25 years. Then what do they do? They raise fines. They increase enforcement. They create new "zones." They extend meter hours. They install new kiosks.

They issue new bonds backed by revenue that is already stretched to the breaking point. This is the classic municipal shell game: Use parking revenue to avoid raising taxes—and ignore the infrastructure that parking revenue was created to serve.

Cities present parking revenue as net-positive income. But the ledger is a lie. Without reinvestment, parking "profit" is actually deferred capital expense. Imagine a landlord who collects rent but never maintains the building. Sure, it looks like profit—until the roof collapses and the repair estimate is $800,000. That's parking. The "profit" evaporates the moment you acknowledge deferred maintenance, structural repair costs, and security upgrades.

Parking revenue does not pay for these things. Eventually, the bill comes due. And the bill is always larger than the accumulated revenue ever was.

Cities that treat parking revenue properly—as a self-funding infrastructure program—experience the opposite trajectory. A well-run parking ecosystem generates stable revenue, safer facilities, better downtown traffic flow and improved retail performance.

This is the operating system that America originally envisioned. It worked—until politics wrecked it. Street parking was never intended to make money. Its purpose is to ensure turnover, prevent vehicles from monopolizing curb space, ensure orderly access, ensure safety and fund off-street parking. Revenue was always the means—not an end in itself.

Once cities began treating curb space as a revenue source rather than a mobility asset, they warped its function. When cities pursue profit instead of access, the curb becomes hostile—and downtown commerce suffers.

What Cities Must Do—The Reinvestment Rule

Every dollar collected from meters, tickets, lots, or parking apps must follow one rule: The Parking Dollar Must Return to the Parking System. Not the general fund. Not the pension deficit. Not a PR campaign. The purpose of parking revenue is singular: build and maintain off-street parking so streets remain safe, functional, and commercially vibrant. Cities that do this thrive. Cities that don't eventually face retail decline, lawsuits/bankruptcies, ratings downgrades, and emergency capital repairs.

Chapter 12

Illegal Parking Revenue Is the LEAST Efficient Funding Mechanism in Government

For decades, city governments have treated parking fines and fees as a harmless source of revenue. A necessary evil. A nuisance tax. The modern equivalent of "sin taxes," except the sin is parking your car near where you live or shop. Officials justify the system by insisting that the money is needed for essential services, and that parking enforcement is simply a tool to maintain "order."

But when you peel back the layers, when you examine the economics, the legal landscape, the bond market, and the psychology of enforcement, a simple truth becomes unavoidable: Illegal parking revenue is the least efficient, most destructive funding mechanism in government.

Let's break down exactly why—financially, legally, ethically, and economically—parking revenue is the single worst dollar a city can collect.

Municipal leaders often claim that parking revenue helps "balance the budget." The numbers tell a different story. Every dollar of parking revenue generates hidden costs, including but not limited to administration, collections/disputes, technology, and infrastructure.

According to the International Parking & Mobility Institute and the Government Accountability Office, in many jurisdictions, when full enforcement, administrative, and dispute costs are accounted for, parking enforcement approaches or exceeds a 1:1 cost-to-revenue ratio, even with all the recent technological advancements over the past decade. A GAO review found that *government-wide fee, fine, and penalty data—including those collected by municipal governments—suffer from significant limitations in availability and oversight.*

Government accountants know this. But the political class hides it because parking revenue looks free. Parking revenue produces no tax revolt—until now. The illusion of efficiency dissolves the moment you ask, "What does it cost to collect a parking dollar versus a sales-tax or property-tax dollar?" The answer in many cases is devastating.

Illegal Parking Revenue Carries Enormous Future Liabilities

Most municipal parking systems in the United States operate on legally fragile ground, whether cities recognize it or not. The reason is simple: parking enforcement depends on lawful notice, and lawful notice depends on compliance with binding standards. The Manual on Uniform Traffic Control Devices (MUTCD) is not guidance or best practice—it is mandatory federal law for traffic control devices on roads open to public travel. When required signs fail MUTCD standards, enforcement tied to those signs collapses. Each defective sign converts what looks like revenue into a contingent liability.

Research conducted under *Operation Parking Takedown* suggests that a substantial majority of municipal parking signs fail at least one mandatory MUTCD requirement. Failures include improper placement, nonstandard colors, inadequate reflectivity, missing legends, conflicting information, and the absence of required regulatory elements. These are not technicalities; they go directly to legal notice. Without lawful notice, enforcement violates due process. Every ticket issued under those conditions becomes a refund waiting to happen.

Cities have unknowingly accumulated what may be among the largest unfunded municipal liabilities in modern history. Invalid parking citations do not disappear simply because they were paid. They remain legally contestable long after issuance, particularly when enforcement defects are systemic rather than incidental. What cities book as revenue is, in reality, deferred debt. Parking income survives only because the liability has not yet been recognized.

This is not speculative. Florida has already seen a version of this movie before. In 2002, the Florida Supreme Court struck down the City of Miami's parking surcharge as an unconstitutional tax, triggering widespread refunds. That case was not about signage or notice, and it is not the theory advanced here. It concerned statutory authority and improper revenue classification. But the result was the same: money cities treated as settled revenue was suddenly reclassified as illegally collected and refundable.

Miami is now facing a similar reckoning again. Current litigation challenges the city's revived parking surcharge on grounds distinct from, but parallel to, the earlier case. If Miami loses—as it did before—the financial consequences could include mass refunds and severe fiscal disruption. The lesson is clear: parking revenue can vanish overnight once courts examine its legal foundation.

The MUTCD-based exposure is potentially far larger than Miami's surcharge problem. Miami's cases involve a discrete charge over a defined period. MUTCD noncompliance implicates every ticket issued under defective notice, often stretching back years or decades. The scope is broader, the refund pool larger, and the liability harder to contain. What Miami faces is a warning; what many cities face is an avalanche.

Chapter 13

The Mirage and the False Economy of Parking Revenue: Impact on Retail Sales and Tourism

Cities often convince themselves that parking revenue is a reliable source of income. Meter rates, app payments, and citations appear to generate steady cash with little obvious political cost. Because the amounts are small and spread across thousands of transactions, the money feels painless. What cities mistake for profit is often just short-term cash flow. The moment long-term costs and economic damage are considered, the revenue vanishes into a mirage.

Parking revenue is only real if it is reinvested directly into the parking system that generated it. Historically, parking funds existed to build, operate, and maintain off-street facilities. When cities followed that model, parking functioned as self-supporting infrastructure. When they abandoned it, parking stopped paying for itself. The illusion of profit replaced actual sustainability.

Once parking revenue began flowing into general funds, incentives changed. Parking policy shifted from access and mobility to extraction and yield. Maintenance was deferred, garages aged, lighting failed, and security declined. The infrastructure parking revenue was meant to support quietly deteriorated. Today's "profit" became tomorrow's emergency capital project.

Cities then attempted to solve that problem the wrong way. Instead of reinvesting, they raised rates, expanded paid hours, intensified enforcement, and increased fines. New zones appeared, kiosks multiplied, and bonds were issued against already-stressed revenue streams. Each step treated parking not as infrastructure, but as a fiscal pressure valve. The shell game has continued until the costs can no longer be hidden.

This is where the false economy becomes visible. Parking revenue is booked in one column, while economic damage appears nowhere on the ledger. Lost foot traffic, shorter visits, reduced retail sales, and declining downtown vitality are not counted. The city sees income, while merchants see emptier sidewalks. That disconnect is what makes parking revenue deceptively attractive.

What should be obvious to everyone has been proven time and again. Multiple independent studies confirm that this dynamic is not anecdotal—it is structural.

Research by Donald Shoup at UCLA shows that higher parking prices and strict enforcement consistently reduce retail visitation by increasing perceived risk and inconvenience, causing shoppers to shorten trips or avoid commercial districts entirely. Analysis by the Victoria Transport Policy Institute found that while parking turnover may improve, overall retail activity and dwell time decline as consumers shift spending to locations with lower parking friction. Municipal data from San Francisco Municipal Transportation Agency SFpark program revealed that blocks with higher prices and intensified enforcement experienced weaker discretionary shopping and lagging sales growth compared to comparable areas. Finally, retail corridor studies by the Urban Land Institute concluded that perceived parking difficulty—confusing rules, app-only payment, and ticket risk—directly suppresses impulse visits and undermines street-level commerce. Across methodologies and cities, the findings align: parking enforcement may generate short-term cash, but it does so by quietly eroding the retail and tourism activity that sustains cities over time.

For example, a place like Palm Beach, where on-street parking now costs seven dollars an hour in certain areas. The town assumes its customers can afford it, and many technically can. But affordability is not the same as willingness. Even affluent consumers respond to friction and perceived hostility. They shorten visits, reduce frequency, or stop coming altogether.

Here's the absolute economic truth no city wants to admit: Paid parking reduces retail sales. Always. Shoppers avoid areas where they risk confusing signs and predatory towing zones. The result? Retail sales drop. Commercial rents fall. Vacancy rises. Small businesses die. Studies from retail economics show that for every 10% increase in parking friction, retail activity falls 3–7%. Cities then panic about the reduced tax base and respond by… increasing parking fines. This is how municipalities create a death spiral and a classic Ponzi dynamic.

A casual stop becomes a conscious transaction. Coffee turns into takeout or drive-thru, shopping becomes browsing online, and lunch becomes delivery. Merchants lose impulse purchases, repeat visits, and dwell time. These losses accumulate quietly and persistently. None of them appear in the city's parking revenue report.

Cities often incredulously misinterpret the resulting decline. When downtown activity slows, officials blame changing consumer habits or e-commerce. Instead of recognizing parking friction as a cause, they increase enforcement to "make up" the difference. That response accelerates the problem rather than fixing it. Parking becomes both the symptom and the driver of decline.

The comparison to malls explains the shift clearly. For decades, people drove farther to shop where parking was free, obvious, and abundant. Consumers learned which environment welcomed them and which punished them. Today, online shopping completes the cycle by eliminating parking altogether.

Parking policy helped train people away from physical commerce. First, they chose malls over downtowns. Then they chose screens over both. Cities that overly monetize curb space unintentionally support and encourage this behavior. The revenue they collect is offset by the economic activity they lose.

This is why cities can lose money on parking even when gross revenue rises. The city captures seven dollars an hour while losing sales tax, business vitality, and long-term occupancy. Vacancies increase, storefronts turn over, and character erodes. Commercial property prices slow down or decline. Turnover of these properties stops and the cities lose transfer taxes and fees many times in excess to the parking charges. The parking "profit" survives only because the losses are externalized and never accounted for.

The final irony is that cities respond tc this damage by raising rates again. When revenue flattens, they assume prices must go higher. They rarely ask whether the revenue problem is self-inflicted. Parking becomes the lever pulled repeatedly, even as the mechanism breaks.

Parking revenue is real only when it supports access rather than taxing presence. When pricing deters people from showing up, the city is not monetizing demand—it is suppressing it. The mirage persists because the damage is delayed, diffuse, and non-identifiable. It's truly a case of the dog that didn't bark. By the time it becomes visible, the system is already entrenched. That is the false economy at the heart of modern parking policy.

Parking is also the most common point of contact people have with local government. Not police. Not zoning inspectors. Not trash collection. Parking enforcement is the daily face of municipal power. When that face is inconsistent, confusing, hostile, impossible to appeal, or run through unaccountable apps, it breeds resentment and distrust. Every unjust ticket writes a silent sentence in the citizen's mind: "My government is not here to serve me—it's here to exploit me." Cities underestimate how corrosive that sentiment is.

Tourism is also affected by illegal parking enforcement. A single ticket in a tourism district does more damage than a hundred marketing ads can repair. Visitors leave with a sense of being preyed upon. Parking enforcement in tourist districts carries outsized reputational risk. A single ticket issued under confusing or unlawful conditions can outweigh millions of dollars in marketing. Visitors leave with the impression that the city is predatory, not welcoming. They share that experience with friends, family, and online audiences.

Tourism depends on frictionless movement and positive memories. Parking enforcement introduces anxiety, uncertainty, and resentment into what should be discretionary leisure spending. Cities then spend heavily trying to repair reputational damage caused by minimal enforcement revenue. The return on that trade is negative.

Just prior to this book being published, I was on Las Olas Boulevard, a very popular tourist district in Fort Lauderdale, Florida. I talked with a couple of out-of-towners while they tried to decipher the confusing parking sign. Since embarking upon this project, I have seen every manner of illegal MUTCD non-compliant sign, but I must admit, this one had me stumped. Finally, they decided that parking was permitted in this zone, although I wasn't sure, and they attempted to pay the fee. They didn't want to use the app because, as one of them expressed, "I don't want 20 parking apps on my phone. And I don't trust them. They are monitoring me and tracking me, and what guarantee do I have that they won't sell my data or that it will be breached?" I couldn't argue with him, so I suggested he buy a copy of my book when it was published.

Legal MUTCD Sign

Fort Lauderdale's Version

Jurisdictions that simplify parking or eliminate paid enforcement in tourist areas consistently see stronger visitation and higher downstream spending. Restaurants, retailers, and service providers benefit immediately. Parking revenue functions as a hidden tax on tourism. Like all poorly designed taxes, it drives demand elsewhere.

Some cities have already demonstrated a better path. Municipalities that do not rely on parking revenue tend to exhibit healthier commercial districts, higher voluntary compliance, and lower administrative friction. They spend less on enforcement, fewer resources on disputes, and far less on litigation. Most importantly, they preserve public trust.

When parking revenue is removed from the general fund equation, budgets rebalance around transparent taxation and accountable spending. Enforcement shifts from extraction to order. Retail stabilizes because customers feel welcome rather than targeted. Bond markets respond favorably to predictable, lawful revenue rather than fragile enforcement schemes.

Parking revenue is often defended as a fiscal necessity, but the evidence suggests the opposite. It introduces instability, legal risk, and long-term economic harm. Cities that move away from it do not decline—they heal. Parking revenue is not a cure for municipal finance. It is a chronic condition that cities have mistaken for medicine.

Chapter 14

Citizens Must Challenge Illegality

This book is a citizen's guide to surviving the Parking Industrial Complex—legally, peacefully, and effectively. Until the lawsuit is filed, litigated, and ultimately victorious—until federal courts confirm what is already evident about the MUTCD, due process, and the unconstitutionality of app-based virtual meters—citizens remain subject to a system that is deeply flawed, often unlawful, and unmistakably predatory. One must live within the law, even when the law is being misapplied. So what can be done in the meantime?

The Reality: 40% of Challenged Parking Tickets Are Dismissed

Across major U.S. cities, roughly 40% of parking tickets that are formally challenged are dismissed or found not liable. Published adjudication data from jurisdictions such as New York City, San Francisco, and Chicago consistently show high failure rates once tickets are subjected to scrutiny. Administrative court statistics from bodies including the New York City Office of Administrative Trials and Hearings and the San Francisco Municipal Transportation Agency point to the same causes again and again: defective signage, procedural errors, and officer mistakes. This is not a marginal problem—it is systemic.

Cities prefer not to advertise this reality. Parking apps bury appeal options deep within menus, while some jurisdictions imply—incorrectly—that tickets are not worth contesting. The system does not depend on accuracy or justice to function. It depends on resignation, time pressure, and attrition.

An even less discussed truth is that cities with aggressive enforcement regimes have spawned a quiet cottage industry: parking ticket fixers. In New York City, major repeat violators such as UPS, FedEx, and large delivery fleets routinely retain specialists whose sole job is to challenge tickets en masse. These fixers succeed at extraordinarily high rates. Over time, the cost of fighting tickets is substantial—but it is still cheaper than paying citations issued by a defective system.

I learned how this system really works the hard way. Years ago, my father received a parking ticket in the mail for a violation that allegedly occurred in Jamaica, Queens. We lived in Essex County, New Jersey, and I can say with certainty that Nat had never parked in Jamaica. I was in law school at the time and volunteered to contest the ticket in person at the New York City Parking Violations Bureau.

What I encountered was not justice—it was an adjudication mill. Dozens of hearings were taking place simultaneously in small rooms throughout the building. I watched professional ticket fixers cycle through cases, having violation after violation dismissed with apparent ease. I assumed my case would be straightforward but was I ever wrong.

When my turn came, I explained that the ticket was not my father's. The make of the car matched, but the registration listed the color as yellow, while the ticket said gold. The hearing officer waved it off: "Gold, yellow—what's the difference?" I pointed out that the ticket listed a four-door vehicle, while my father's car had two doors. "Two doors, four doors—that's immaterial," he said. Growing frustrated, I noted that the ticket did not even list the vehicle's year. To my surprise, the hearing officer paused and said, "That's material. Ticket dismissed."

I was stunned. The one fact a meter enforcement officer is least likely to know—the model year of a vehicle—was the only detail deemed legally significant. Everything else, including obvious mismatches, was brushed aside. I accepted the win, but the logic behind the policy has never stopped bothering me. That is how mass adjudication works in large cities: not by truth, but by procedural thresholds designed for throughput.

Always remember this: the law is clear. When signs are not MUTCD-compliant, when notice is inadequate, and when virtual meters replace required physical infrastructure, citations cannot stand. The high dismissal rate is not an anomaly—it is the system quietly admitting its own defects.

The MUTCD Is Your Shield

If a ticket is received, the proper response is lawful and straightforward:

1. Return to the location immediately.
2. Photograph the sign from every relevant angle.
3. Capture its height, obstructions, visibility, and the entire block context.
4. Compare the sign to MUTCD Chapter 2B requirements.
5. Submit a challenge through the app's hidden appeal pathway.
6. Attach the photos.
7. State clearly and succinctly:

"This sign is not compliant with the MUTCD and therefore cannot form the basis of a lawful citation."

No emotion. No argument about fairness. Simply invoke the federal standard.

Cities know they cannot defend non-compliant signage. They know a legal precedent against them would destroy the parking revenue model. My own ticket—which gave rise to this book, this movement, and this lawsuit—was tossed for this very reason. Most first-tier reviews are automated. However, when the MUTCD is invoked with photographic evidence, the default outcome is dismissal.

If you join the NAADP, the National Association of American Defrauded Parkers, you will receive a parking ticket self-defense kit that will help you create a defense that even the most flippant, cynical, hardcore New York City Parking adjudicator will find difficult to refuse.

One caveat: TOW-AWAY Zones. When they have your car, your heart and mind will follow. Always remember, never ever risk a tow. Some jurisdictions, like New York City, are citywide tow-away zones. Even when citizens are right on the law, the vehicle will be impounded first and questioned later. Elsewhere, towing is rare, giving citizens more flexibility. Use judgment. No legal stand is worth losing a vehicle.

The 90-Day Strategy: Lawful Assertion of Rights

This is not civil disobedience. This is not protest. This is lawful participation in the process that cities themselves created. If every driver who receives a ticket over the next ninety days photographs the sign, cites the MUTCD, refuses the first denial, and pushes the case to second-tier review, then the system will choke on its own administrative burden.

Not because citizens broke the rules—but because they followed the law, the actual law, more diligently than the municipalities themselves. You will be fulfilling the promise of the *Dunleavy Doctrine* that extractive systems always fail when they are forced to follow their own rules.

This book does not advocate ignoring parking regulations. It advocates awareness, documentation, lawful challenge, and insisting on MUTCD compliance.

This book is Exhibit A in a lawsuit that we hope will reshape American parking enforcement. But until that day arrives, citizens still have rights, and the MUTCD remains the supreme standard. Use it. Because when enough people insist that the government follow its own rules, the Parking Industrial Complex collapses—not from rebellion, but from accountability.

15

You Can't Not Fight City Hall

"You can't fight City Hall." It's one of those sayings that sounds like wisdom because it has been repeated for generations. A shrug disguised as experience, passed along as friendly advice. Don't bother. Don't resist. Just pay and move on. For a long time, that phrase worked precisely because people believed it.

That belief trained citizens to see local government as immovable and inevitable. It taught people to tolerate small injustices rather than confront them. It framed resistance as naive and compliance as maturity. But today, that saying is no longer just wrong—it is actively dangerous. The cost of believing it has grown too high.

City Hall is no longer a quiet building where clerks shuffle paper and councils argue over street repairs. It has become a revenue system, an enforcement platform, and a data operation embedded into daily life. Its reach is constant, automated, and largely invisible. The harm it causes is no longer occasional or accidental. It is systemic and deliberate. If people do not fight City Hall now, they may not get another chance.

Local government used to be boring by design. It was meant to be visible, limited, and accountable. Parking enforcement meant a sign, a meter, and a human being writing a ticket in plain sight. Errors were obvious and contestable. Abuse existed, but friction kept it contained.

Technology removed that friction. What began as convenience turned into automation. Automation evolved into optimization, and optimization became monetization. Monetization inevitably turned into extraction. Each step was justified by claims of efficiency, even as accountability quietly disappeared.

Cities learned an uncomfortable truth along the way. Raising money through fines and fees is easier than raising taxes. Taxes require votes, public debate, and political risk. Fees slip through quietly, labeled as regulation or compliance. Parking, code enforcement, and administrative penalties became ideal tools.

City Hall did not become corrupt overnight. It became dependent. Local power is uniquely dangerous because it feels familiar. It governs the curb, the sidewalk, the driveway, and the routines of everyday life. Because the harm arrives in small increments, people lower their guard. A ticket here and a fee there do not feel like tyranny. Over time, however, they add up to something much larger.

A parking ticket does not feel like oppression. A code violation does not feel like a constitutional issue. A convenience fee does not feel like a civil liberties problem. But multiplied across thousands of transactions and enforced by software and algorithms, these small impositions become systemic abuse. The scale is what changes everything.

Most people do not fight City Hall because the system is designed to make resistance irrational. The fine is low enough that paying feels easier than contesting. The appeal process is confusing and time-consuming by design. The threat of escalation—late fees, collections, towing—creates fear. Rational people respond by complying.

This is not accidental. It is behavioral design. Modern enforcement does not rely on fairness or persuasion. It relies on math and probability. New York City provides the clearest window into how parking enforcement actually functions at scale. Through its administrative court system, the NYC Office of Administrative Trials and Hearings, the city processes more than 10 million parking tickets each year! Official reports show that only about 3–4% of those citations are ever formally challenged (a remarkable 300,000 to 400,000 cases per year), despite their enormous volume. Yet when motorists do contest tickets, as many as 45% get dismissed. The most common reasons include defective or confusing signage, incorrect location or time entries, procedural errors, and officer mistakes. The implication is unavoidable: a substantial share of parking tickets do not withstand scrutiny, but the system depends on the fact that almost no one challenges them. Parking enforcement in New York is not optimized for accuracy or justice; it is optimized for resignation.

If ninety-six out of one hundred people pay quietly, the system succeeds. Whether the rule was clear or lawful becomes secondary. Volume overwhelms justice. Now imagine if 15% of ticketed motorists showed up to fight. That would mean nearly 1,500,000 hearings would be required. No system can handle that volume.

This is why "pay and go away" has become the real law of the curb. The system does not need to be right. It only needs to be inconvenient to challenge. Once people internalize that logic, resistance collapses. Compliance becomes automatic. What has changed—and why the old saying no longer applies—is evidence. Citizens can now document abuse at scale. Phones capture illegal signs and missing notice. Apps record failures and inconsistencies. Public records expose revenue dependence.

Courts do not think in anecdotes. They think in patterns and systems. Once a judge sees that enforcement is not about safety or cost recovery, but about predictable revenue, the narrative shifts. Legal justifications begin to weaken. The system's true purpose becomes visible.

Local fights matter more than national ones because they are concrete. A sign exists, or it does not. A rate was raised, or it was not. Revenue went to the general fund, or it did not. These are verifiable facts, not political opinions. Cities appear powerful, but they are brittle. They rely on bond ratings, predictable cash flow, and public trust. They fear injunctions, discovery, and sustained scrutiny. When exposed, they retreat. When challenged persistently, they compromise.

This is not about parking. Parking is simply where the abuse became visible. It is where ordinary people encountered a system that no longer made sense. It is where law quietly gave way to software. And it is where the fight necessarily begins. This is about whether local government still serves the public or quietly treats citizens as revenue sources. It is about whether the law is posted clearly or embedded invisibly in code. It is about whether compliance replaces consent. Those questions extend far beyond the curb.

When citizens stop challenging small injustices, larger ones follow naturally. When systems learn that people will always pay rather than resist, limits disappear. Power expands to fill silence. What goes unchallenged becomes normalized. Fighting City Hall is not radical. It is foundational. Every major reform in American history began locally, not nationally. Change starts when ordinary people refuse to accept inevitability.

Civil rights, property rights, and due process did not emerge from resignation. They emerged from resistance that was initially dismissed as futile. The same warning was given then: you can't fight City Hall. History proved otherwise.

It does not require chaos or spectacle. It requires documentation, persistence, and refusal to accept explanations unsupported by facts. It means asking where the money goes and demanding proof when rates rise. It means understanding that silence is consent. "You can't fight City Hall" was never a statement of fact. It was a statement of convenience. It protected those in power by discouraging those without it. That lie only works if people keep repeating it until they believe it.

The Cities Have No Defense

For decades, cities across America have engaged in the quiet, lucrative, and legally indefensible business of issuing parking tickets based on signs that violate federal law. These violations aren't occasional. They are systematic, widespread, structural, and unavoidable. They sit in plain sight—literally bolted into metal poles on every block—and they expose municipalities to a level of liability that most city officials still refuse to contemplate.

Yet when confronted with these MUTCD violations—failures in clarity, visibility, reflectivity, legibility, placement, mounting height, directional arrows, panel combinations, contrast ratios, and required sign families—cities retreat to the same tired, hopeless excuse: "We didn't know." Not only is that false. It is impossible. And legally, it is irrelevant.

They cannot claim ignorance. They cannot feign confusion. They cannot plead "we didn't realize" in front of a judge. Their actions were not accidents. They were policy choices. Sign vendors, engineering firms, consultants, and parking technology companies all understand MUTCD requirements. They market compliance. They certify compliance. They charge for compliance. They write proposals promising MUTCD adherence.

The idea that a city "did not know" is as absurd as a doctor claiming he did not know that he needed a medical license. They knew. They just didn't care. The courts have long stated that governments are bound by their own laws and cannot benefit from violating them. Whether it is improper notice, defective ordinances, illegitimate signage, or unconstitutional procedures, municipalities lose when they fail to comply with their own standards.

Due process requires lawful notice. Unlawful signs cannot provide notice. Therefore, unlawful signs cannot support enforcement. Ignorance is irrelevant. Compliance is mandatory. Here is the darkest part of the entire parking scam: The cities profited from their own misconduct. Every MUTCD violation produced more ticket, towing, booting revenue, and app commissions.

When a government profits from violating federal law, the legal burden on that government skyrockets. A city cannot break federal law, punish the citizen, and profit from the violation. And then claim, "We didn't know." That is the definition of bad faith government conduct. If municipalities wanted to avoid liability, they had one option: Fix the signs. Not argue. Not rationalize. Not stonewall. Not enrich parking vendors. Not punish residents.

Just comply with the law that every American driver is expected to obey. Instead, they constructed a shadow economy of parking revenue bonds, enforcement quotas, digital ticketing systems, surveillance programs, and app-based payment schemes—all built on illegal signs.

When evaluating government conduct, courts use a stricter lens. A private citizen may claim ignorance. A government cannot. Why? Because a government has infinite access to legal counsel, control over the regulatory environment, and a responsibility to protect constitutional rights.

With great power comes great responsibility. Cities wield enormous power over the daily lives of their residents—the power to ticket, tow, fine, boot, and penalize. With that power comes the nonnegotiable duty to follow the law. Their failure is not an accident. It is a breach of public trust.

Cities often justify their noncompliance by pointing to other cities:

"Everyone uses these signs."

"Everyone has similar meters."

"Everyone stacks panels like this."

"Everyone uses the same vendors."

This reasoning fails for one simple reason: Illegality does not become legal through repetition. Uniform wrongdoing is still wrongdoing. In fact, it is the definition of a scheme. The Constitution demands clear notice, fair warning, and lawful enforcement. Due process was never optional. Cities violated each of these by enforcing illegal signage. You cannot give due process if the underlying law was never followed by the enforcer.

Cities deprived millions of Americans of due process, one ticket at a time. They cannot shrug and say "Oops." This is not a parking issue. It is a constitutional issue. Once federal noncompliance is exposed publicly and judicially, cities will face class actions, refund liability, bond disclosure investigations, ADA exposure, vendor lawsuits and bankruptcy. And none of it will be defensible under the excuse of "we did not know." Cities had decades to comply. They chose not to. Now the bill is due.

When the Parking Takedown begins its formal legal assault, cities will scramble to adopt any defensive posture they can. They will blame vendors, blame engineers, blame contractors, blame past administrations, blame the public, blame the weather—anything but themselves. But the truth will cut through it: Ignorance is no defense—especially for government. Compliance was mandatory. The violations were obvious. And the profit was intentional.

The cities have no defense. Not legally. Not morally. They built an empire on unlawful signs, and now the entire structure is collapsing.

Chapter 16

How Parking is Done Across the United States

America is a country built on regional differences. Clam chowder in the Northeast tastes nothing like gumbo in the South. The vowels of Boston don't resemble those of Birmingham. What no one talks about is that parking enforcement is just as regionally diverse, and often just as messy, spicy, or terrifying as the local cuisine. America's parking regimes form a cultural tapestry—a quilt sewn with punitive revenue, fear, fiscal desperation, and federally non-compliant signage. And like any true American tradition, none of it makes sense. (Ticket fees subject to change.)

The Northeast—"Where Sanity Goes to Die"

New York City is the undisputed heavyweight champion of enforcement madness. Tickets range from $65–$115 and higher, always higher. Towing: $185 + storage + administrative fees.

On-street parking is disappearing faster than the middle class.

In many neighborhoods, the city has eliminated entire stretches of legal parking and converted curb lanes into loading zones, bike lanes, or "pilot programs."

The result is that illegal parking is no longer a choice—it is a survival tactic.

As for off-street parking? NYC has some of the most expensive garages on Earth:

- Midtown: $65–$90 for 2 hours
- Luxury garages: $800–$1,200 per month

It is legitimately cheaper to park a Boeing 747 overnight at JFK than a Honda Civic in Tribeca.

Boston—The Puritan Doctrine of Parking Sin

Boston enforces parking like a Calvinist enforcing moral law:

- $55–$120 fines
- Zero forgiveness

Parking in Boston isn't illegal—it's heretical.

Philadelphia—The Most Absurd Regime in America

The Philadelphia Parking Authority (PPA) is what happens when enforcement, ego, entrepreneurship, and chaos merge into one blue-and-white boot-wielding organism.

The South—"Gentle Accents, Aggressive Towing"

Atlanta—Sweet Tea & Surprise Boots

Cheap tickets ($25–$50), but tow trucks circulate with NASCAR enthusiasm.

New Orleans—Enforcement by Voodoo

Rules appear and disappear depending on moon phase, mood, or who won the Saints game. Your car might be towed "for safety reasons," which means: they felt like moving it and won't explain why.

The Midwest—"Reasonable Until It Isn't"

Chicago—The Red-Light-Camera State

- Tickets: $50–$150
- Booting after 3 unpaid tickets

The Mountain West—"The Booting Badlands"

Denver invented the modern wheel boot in the 1950s, and they remain spiritually committed to it.

The West Coast—"Enforcement by Zen Torture"

San Francisco—The Vatican of Parking Apostasy

- $70–$120 tickets
- $575+ towing
- $110 street-cleaning fines
- $7/hr meters

Parking in SF is a spiritual stripping of ego, dignity, and wealth.

Los Angeles—Signs by Sorcery

Five signs stacked on one pole, each contradicting the last. Legal Jenga everywhere.

The Plains—"The Last Frontier of Parking Innocence"

Some towns still issue:

- $5 tickets
- 25¢ per hour meters
- $2/day lots

These towns are America's last living parking utopias.

America's regional parking traditions are inconsistent, illogical, improvisational, predatory, occasionally charming, and always expensive. But beneath the diversity lies one unifying truth: Most signage is illegal, non-MUTCD compliant, and unenforceable—which is why the Parking Reformation is coming for them.

Chapter 17

Chicago: The Special Case

Chicago occupies a unique position in the modern parking enforcement landscape because it did not merely regulate parking—it financialized it. By leasing its parking meters to a private concessionaire, the city converted routine curbside regulation into a long-dated revenue instrument backed by continuous enforcement. The deal assumed that parking rules would remain enforceable, predictable, and legally sound for decades. Unlike other cities, Chicago cannot easily change or forgive parking practices without triggering financial consequences. That structural dependency makes Chicago different in kind, not degree.

The city's history provides essential context. Chicago has long been associated with machine politics, patronage, and public-private arrangements that blur the line between governance and monetization. Parking enforcement fits squarely within that tradition, evolving from a regulatory function into a revenue discipline protected by contracts and assumptions. The parking meter deal followed this pattern, locking future administrations into obligations negotiated under earlier political regimes. What appears today as rigid enforcement is often the downstream consequence of those legacy arrangements.

Under the current system, parking tickets are issued by city employees and processed through municipal administrative tribunals, giving them the outward appearance—and often the reality—of legal force. Yet the economic beneficiary of widespread compliance is no longer solely the public, but private investors who recovered their capital early and continue to collect ongoing cash flow. This creates a bifurcated system: strict enforcement for ordinary drivers, and quiet flexibility for those who know how to navigate it. The legality of a ticket depends entirely on the validity of the underlying restriction and the adequacy of notice, not on the volume of tickets written.

That imbalance is illustrated by my doctor brother-in-law, a habitual scofflaw who collected parking tickets the way others collect coupons. He routinely ignored restrictions, accumulated large outstanding balances, and treated enforcement as a nuisance rather than a deterrent. Yet through a fixer attorney who understood the system, those tickets were ultimately resolved for a pittance compared to their face value. His experience demonstrates that the system is neither uniformly punitive nor uniformly just—it is selectively forgiving to those with access and opaque to those without.

Chicago's reliance on complex signage, calendar-based restrictions, permit zones, and app-mediated explanations reinforces this selectivity. The Manual on Uniform Traffic Control Devices exists to ensure that parking rules are clear, standardized, and immediately intelligible to ordinary drivers. When legality depends on consulting an app, a website, or insider local knowledge, notice has already failed. Apps cannot cure defective signs; they merely monetize ambiguity downstream. In a securitized enforcement system, that ambiguity becomes a feature rather than a flaw.

Mayor Brandon Johnson has publicly expressed interest in bringing Chicago's parking meters back under public control, a position that would have been unthinkable when the deal was first signed. That interest reflects a widely acknowledged reality: the private consortium recovered its initial investment extraordinarily quickly, with substantial cash flow continuing long after. The political problem is not desire, but mechanism—Chicago cannot unwind the deal without either paying dearly or demonstrating that the revenue stream itself is legally impaired. If parking enforcement rests on defective notice, non-compliant signage, or unlawful substitution of apps for traffic control devices, that impairment becomes structural rather than discretionary. In that sense, this book and the accompanying litigation may unintentionally provide the very off-ramp the city has lacked.

If Chicago's parking signs or app-based enforcement mechanisms are ultimately found non-compliant under governing standards, the consequences extend far beyond individual tickets. Revenue streams assumed to be stable become impaired, enforcement actions lose their legal foundation, and the concession itself becomes structurally unstable. This is why Chicago cannot quietly reform its parking system the way other cities might. The city sold not just meters, but certainty, and certainty depends on lawful notice. In that sense, Chicago is not merely a bad example; it is the stress test.

If this system ultimately collapses under legal scrutiny, the ramifications are likely to be neither quick nor clean. The creation, monetization, and sale of an unlawful enforcement regime raises questions that extend to force majeure, impossibility of performance, and the allocation of risk when foundational assumptions fail. What follows would not be a single lawsuit, but a cascade—administrative challenges, contract disputes, investor claims, and municipal defenses stretching over a decade or more. That outcome would surprise no one familiar with Chicago's long history as the nation's proving ground for municipal corruption and transactional governance. When a city builds and sells a system on ambiguity, prolonged litigation is not an accident—it is the inevitable unwind.

Chapter 18

How the World Parks and Extracts

How The World Screws You, And Why America Is the Only Place Where Illegal Enforcement Can Be Brought Down

Across the planet, curb space has become a battleground. Every nation has created its own version of the parking enforcement machine—some bureaucratic, some brutal, some casually indifferent, and some engineered with near-military precision. Yet only in the United States does a unique and powerful vulnerability exist: the ability to challenge illegal enforcement using federal uniformity standards, due process requirements, and constitutional law.

SINGAPORE—THE SURVEILLANCE-PUNISHMENT REGIME

Singapore has built the most unforgiving parking system in the world. Enforcement utilizes real-time electronic parking systems (EPS), ubiquitous license-plate scanning with automated fines issued instantly.

Their philosophy is simple: compliance through certainty, intensity, and omnipresent monitoring. Parking management is not treated as a convenience or revenue stream—it is a behavioral control mechanism.

Singapore also maintains one of the world's few remaining systems of judicial caning. While parking violations themselves do not lead to corporal punishment, the existence of caning as a lawful penalty for other offenses shapes the national psychology.

Certain crimes can still result in ten lashes of rattan cane, administered by trained specialists whose work serves as a reminder that rule-breaking in Singapore carries real consequences. The cultural effect is unmistakable: when citizens receive a parking ticket for being seven inches over a line, they pay it without protest.

The awareness that the state is willing and able to enforce rules with uncompromising severity ensures obedience. The regime achieves through fear what many nations attempt through fines alone.

UNITED KINGDOM—THE BUREAUCRATIC KAFKA MODEL

The United Kingdom enforces parking through an elaborate system of civil penalties (PCNs), private parking firms operating under contract and Automated Number Plate Recognition (ANPR) cameras.

British parking law is dense, contradictory, and often inscrutable. Signs vary widely, rules shift from borough to borough, and enforcement is both relentless and humorless. The system functions through bureaucratic fatigue: most people pay rather than navigate the Byzantine labyrinth of appeal tribunals. This model is not built on illegal enforcement; it is built on the idea that the process itself is punishment.

GERMANY—THE TEUTONIC ORDER MODEL

Germany's system emphasizes clarity, uniformity, and predictability. Signs are precise, regulations are strictly followed, and enforcement is rational rather than revenue-driven. German cities do not use parking policy as a financial instrument. The result is a system that produces high compliance without manipulation, confusion, or predatory tactics.

JAPAN—THE ZEN OF COMPLIANCE

Japan approaches parking with a cultural commitment to order and achieves compliance through clarity and shared norms, not exploitation. The combination of highly accurate signage and respectful but firm enforcement makes it a model of what MUTCD intended U.S. cities to be.

FRANCE—THE CASUAL ANARCHY MODEL

France displays wide variability in parking behavior. Outside Paris, enforcement is inconsistent and often disregarded. Sidewalk parking, median parking, and improvised parking are common. France's parking culture is shaped more by social norms than by enforcement infrastructure.

CANADA—THE POLITE AMBUSH

Canada maintains relatively clear signage and consistent application of rules, especially in major urban centers. Towing is aggressive, but fines are generally lower than in the U.S. Importantly, Canadian jurisdictions often void tickets when signage is inadequate—an approach that contrasts sharply with American municipal resistance to accountability.

AUSTRALIA—THE "FAIR BUT FIRM" SYSTEM

Australian parking enforcement closely resembles the U.K. model but applies clearer signage and more predictable rules. Crucially, Australian tribunals routinely cancel tickets when signs do not meet legal standards. In other words, Australia does what American cities claim to do—but often don't.

WHY AMERICA IS UNIQUE

Among all global parking regimes, only the United States possesses:

1. A federal manual governing signage (MUTCD)
2. Constitutional due process protections
3. Tens of millions of noncompliant signs
4. Municipal dependence on illegal enforcement
5. Legal pathways for citizens to challenge unlawful practices
6. A judiciary capable of striking down defective systems
7. A public fed up with predatory fines
8. A federalist structure that allows national reform through local precedent

This creates a perfect storm: a system built on illegality that can be dismantled through litigation, documentation, and public scrutiny.

Once illegal enforcement is exposed and challenged successfully, American parking policy will undergo a transformation. Other nations will observe this shift closely, but none are positioned to replicate it. The battle against illegal municipal enforcement can only be fought—and won—on American soil. The global parking landscape proves one thing: abusive systems are everywhere, but only in the United States does the legal framework exist to dismantle them.

Chapter 19

The Parkerville Parking Extraction Engine

Following the Money: Parkerville's Parking P&L They Pray You'll Never See

Below is a realistic, conservative Profit & Loss Statement for a mid-sized *hypothetical* Florida city—Parkerville, population 100,000—with modern parking enforcement, mandatory parking apps, and statutory conflicts baked into daily operations.

ANNUAL REVENUE (Extracted Directly from Residents and Visitors)

Kiosk/Meter/App Revenues	$4,200,000
Parking Citations (Tickets)	3,600,000
Late Fees & Penalties	1,100,000
Residential & Commercial Perits	1,000,000
Special Event Parking	350,000
Towing & Impound Rebates (Kickbacks)	750,000
Collection Agency Recoveries	300,000
Total Revenue	11,300,000
Expenses (Feeding the Machine)	
Payroll & Benefits	2,435,000
Equipment, Apps & Infrastructure	2,150,000
Enforcement Costs	135,000
Overhead	1,325,000
Total Expenses	7,260,000
Net Surplus	$ 4,040,000
Loss to merchants, tourist losses non-economic losses and town reputation	**Priceless**

Parking Apps—Parkerville's Hidden Cut of Convenience Fees

Florida statute §215.322 allows municipalities to charge only the actual cost of credit card acceptance —nothing more. But every app used in Florida cities charges flat fees that equate to 8–20% of the parking amount. This is far above any MFN (Most Favored Nation) credit-card rate cities receive (typically 1.4–2.0%).

ParkMobile discloses its exorbitant fees. In PayByPhone hides its fees entirely, simply providing a total payment inclusive of its fee. Yet cities claim the fees are charged by the app, and the app claims the fees are for the city—a circular delegation with no statutory basis. In return for these fees, the Apps provide the cities valuable tools, including, free enforcement dashboards, enforcement agent route optimization, expired meter alerts, violation-probability heat maps, and behavioral analytics designed to maximize extraction.

The Florida Problem

Florida law explicitly prohibits municipalities from charging any fee above their actual credit card acceptance cost. Cities negotiate MFN (most favored nation status) rates that guarantee the lowest processing fees available to any equivalent governmental entity. Thus, any fee above the actual out-of-pocket amount is unlawful.

The exhibits included show actual Florida app transactions:

My receipts show the following fees charged by different Florida Cities. Park Mobile presumably pays the same fee to the credit card processor and yet the fee charged ranges from $0.35 to $0.45

- Boca Raton: $0.40 fee
- Delray Beach: $0.45 fee recently raised from $0.35
- Palm Beach: $0.40
- West Palm Beach: $0.40
- Miami Beach $0.35
- Fort Lauderdale: not shown on receipt

Not much, until one considers the percentage 7–2%, depending upon the number of hours parked.

According to Park Mobile on their site, "Transaction fees are charged per parking transaction and per parking extension, based on where you park. Not all parking providers charge a transaction fee in addition to posted parking rates; some parking providers waive the transaction fee."

Conclusion

If you found this book shocking and somewhat upsetting, then I have done my job. My intent was not solely to outrage—but to help you gain an understanding of the mechanics of *America's Great Parking Scam*, and to see more clearly the relationship between citizens, government, and the increasingly sophisticated devices used to separate you from your hard-earned cash, on swipe at a time.

For far too long, the public has been docile and compliant. For far too long, predatory practices have masqueraded as "administration," "modernization," or "regulation." And for far too long, an unconstitutional, unlawful, and fundamentally immoral system has gone unchallenged simply because most people never knew they had the right to fight back.

That ends now!

It is time to take a stand—peacefully, lawfully, and effectively—and insist that your town, your city, your county, and your state be held accountable for the rules they are required to follow. The MUTCD is not optional. Notice is not optional. Due process is not optional. And the government is not exempt from the law simply because enforcing it upon themselves is inconvenient.

The truth is simple: If just 10% of the motoring public who receive parking violation notices assert their lawful rights, the system will be forced to yield. No city in America is equipped to withstand that level of legitimate, organized, lawful resistance. Their model depends entirely on quiet compliance. Once the public stops complying automatically, the machine stalls.

And if the lawsuit for which this book serves as Exhibit A concludes successfully, then every other effort to hold the system accountable will become moot. The structure itself will be overturned—and every municipality in America will be required to follow federal law, or abandon these predatory practices entirely.

Enter The NAADP

Most Americans don't realize they're part of a class until the bill shows up. Parking enforcement was designed to feel small, fragmented, and personal—just another nuisance you deal with and move on from. A ticket here, a fee there, a surcharge you barely notice until it compounds. That design is intentional because systems of extraction survive by keeping people isolated. No one fights back over twenty-five dollars.

The truth is that parking has quietly become one of the largest unregulated consumer-extraction systems in America. It now operates at the intersection of municipal finance, private vendors, surveillance technology, and administrative law. What looks like traffic management on the surface is often revenue engineering underneath. Once cities discovered parking could be monetized, securitized, and automated, the purpose fundamentally changed. The driver became the product.

That is why the National Association of American Defrauded Parkers (NAADP) was founded. Not by lobbyists, not by politicians, and not by anyone with a financial interest in parking enforcement. It was created because tens of millions of Americans are being fined, tracked, coerced, and taxed through systems that often fail basic legal and regulatory standards. Individually, no one has leverage. Collectively, the leverage is enormous.

NAADP exists to convert individual frustration into collective standing. Cities can ignore a single angry driver with one offensive citation, but they cannot ignore masses of aggrieved parkers with patterns documented at scale. Regulators dismiss anecdotes, but they respond to coordinated complaints supported by evidence. Journalists may overlook one bad ticket, but they pay attention to systemic abuse. NAADP provides the structure that turns noise into signal.

This organization is not anti-parking, anti-order, or anti-city. It is anti-fraud, anti-coercion, and anti-extraction disguised as regulation. When parking rules are clear, lawful, properly signed, and fairly enforced, compliance happens naturally. When signs are illegal, fees masquerade as taxes, apps are mandatory, and appeals are procedural traps, resistance is justified. NAADP draws that line very clearly and unapologetically.

One of NAADP's core missions is to expose non-compliant signage. Parking signs are not suggestions; they are legal instruments that must meet federal and state standards. When they do not, they fail to create enforceable violations. This fact alone undermines thousands of tickets issued every day. Most drivers are unaware of this, and cities count on their ignorance.

Another mission is challenging the widespread abuse of so-called "fees." Across the country, municipalities label taxes as fees to avoid voter approval and legislative authority. Courts have repeatedly ruled that the substance of a charge matters more than its label. Parking has become a favored workaround because it is politically quiet and administratively easy. NAADP exists to force that issue back into the open.

NAADP also investigates app-based parking enforcement and the data practices that accompany it. Many drivers, often minors, are coerced into using apps that collect location and behavioral data, often without meaningful alternatives. These systems blur the line between payment convenience and surveillance infrastructure. When enforcement depends on apps, choice disappears. NAADP treats that as a rights issue, not a technical one.

Perhaps most importantly, NAADP targets parking revenue securitization. Once parking revenue is pledged to bondholders, enforcement priorities shift from public service to debt service. Ticket volume, fee escalation, and aggressive collection stop being accidents and start being requirements. The machine must be fed, regardless of legality or fairness. That is where public policy quietly gives way to financial obligation.

The reason this system resists scrutiny is simple: organization is dangerous to it. Millions of disconnected drivers are manageable. A unified body documenting abuse, coordinating challenges, and creating visibility is not. NAADP makes patterns impossible to ignore and narratives harder to control. That alone explains much of the silence surrounding parking reform.

If you have ever paid a ticket that you knew was wrong, missed a sign that was unreadable or contradictory, been forced into an app you didn't want, or been denied a meaningful appeal, you are already part of this story. Joining NAADP does not require you to sue anyone or spend your days fighting city hall. It simply means your experience is counted instead of being buried. Scale is the difference between grievance and reform.

This book exists because parking drifted far from its original purpose. NAADP exists because silence has become more expensive than speaking. Once enough people are counted, the system loses its invisibility. And systems that depend on invisibility do not survive exposure.

Just go to www.PayandgoAway.com and subscribe to our Substack, which is the home of the NAADP

We pledge to stop any app, authority, consultant, or bond covenant from superseding the rights, dignity, and mobility of the citizenry.

Appendix A

Federal Authority, MUTCD Compliance, and Parking Enforcement

Federal Authority and the MUTCD

The Manual on Uniform Traffic Control Devices (MUTCD) derives its binding legal authority from federal law. Under 23 C.F.R. § 655.603, the MUTCD is adopted as the national standard for all traffic control devices installed on any street, highway, or facility open to public travel. Each state is required to adopt the MUTCD, or a compliant state version, as a condition of receiving federal highway funds. Municipalities are bound through the state's acceptance of those funds, regardless of whether the municipality itself directly receives federal money.

Uniformity is not optional. Congress deliberately tied traffic control standards to federal funding to prevent local governments from creating confusing, inconsistent, or revenue-driven enforcement schemes. The MUTCD exists to ensure that traffic rules are recognizable, predictable, and uniformly applied across jurisdictions. When a city departs from those standards, the consequences are legal as well as practical: unenforceable citations, due process violations, and potential exposure to funding and liability risk.

What Qualifies as a Traffic Control Device

Parking enforcement turns on a single threshold question: is the sign a lawful traffic control device? The MUTCD answers that question clearly, but only when read as a system rather than through isolated quotations.

A traffic control device is defined as a sign, signal, marking, or other device placed by authority of a public body for the purpose of regulating, warning, or guiding traffic. That authority, however, is conditional. A device qualifies as a lawful traffic control device only if it conforms to MUTCD standards governing design, placement, uniformity, and legibility. A sign that does not meet those standards is not a lawful traffic control device, regardless of where it is placed or who erected it. This distinction is critical. Enforcement authority flows from the device itself, not from the pole, curb, or municipal ordinance behind it. When a sign fails MUTCD compliance, enforcement based on that sign constitutes enforcement without valid notice.

Mandatory Compliance and Uniformity

The MUTCD leaves no discretion on compliance. Traffic control devices must conform to the Manual. In MUTCD terminology, the word "shall" denotes a mandatory requirement, not a guideline or best practice. This requirement applies to all regulatory signs, including parking restrictions, time limits, payment conditions, and enforcement rules.

Uniformity is a core principle of the MUTCD. Devices must meet the needs of all road users and simplify comprehension rather than increase cognitive burden. Parking systems that assume smartphone ownership, QR-code literacy, app downloads, data plans, or real-time connectivity violate the uniformity requirement by design. A system that only works for a subset of users is not uniform, and a non-uniform system cannot serve as lawful notice.

Regulatory Parking Signs and the R7 Series

Parking signs are regulatory signs governed by Chapter 2B of the MUTCD, including the R7 series. These signs regulate parking permissions, restrictions, time limits, and conditions of use. As regulatory signs, they must clearly state the rule, stand alone as notice, and use standardized legends, colors, shapes, and formatting.

While payment methods may be supplemented by additional information, the regulatory rule itself must appear on the sign. A sign that defers essential terms to a QR code, mobile application, or website does not provide lawful notice and does not qualify as a compliant regulatory sign. Technology may facilitate payment, but it may not substitute for regulatory disclosure.

Applicability to Municipal Lots, Garages, and Parking Authorities

The MUTCD applies to any facility open to public travel, including municipal parking lots, garages, and parking structures. What governmental entity claims ownership is irrelevant. Public access is the controlling factor. Parking authorities, whether organized as departments, enterprises, or quasi-independent entities, exercise delegated police power and are fully bound by MUTCD requirements.

A municipality cannot evade federal uniformity requirements by outsourcing enforcement to a parking authority or private vendor. If the public is invited to park and citations are issued, the MUTCD applies. Public parking facilities are not constitutional or regulatory free zones.

Legal Consequences of Non-Compliance

A non-compliant sign is not a lawful traffic control device. Citations issued based on such signs are legally defective because they rest on invalid notice. This principle applies equally to streets, lots, garages, and authority-operated facilities.

Parking enforcement depends on lawful traffic control devices. Under MUTCD §§ 1A.01, 1A.02, and 1A.13, a sign that does not conform to MUTCD standards is not a valid traffic control device and cannot create an enforceable parking obligation. This conclusion is conservative, well-supported, and consistent with the structure and purpose of the MUTCD.

When enforcement proceeds without lawful devices, the issue is not technical noncompliance. It is enforcement without authority.

Appendix B

State Adoption of the MUTCD—Parking Enforcement Applicability

All four states below have already adopted the MUTCD or a state MUTCD in substantial conformance with the federal MUTCD. That adoption governs all regulatory traffic control devices, including parking signs, wherever parking is enforced by citation.

Florida

- Florida Statutes § 316.0745—Uniform Signals and Devices

Requires the Florida Department of Transportation (FDOT) to adopt a uniform system of traffic control devices and mandates that all official traffic control devices installed by any public body conform to that system.

- Florida Administrative Code Rule 14-15.010

Formally adopts the Federal MUTCD by reference as Florida's Manual on Uniform Traffic Control Devices.

Effect: All parking signs installed and enforced by Florida municipalities must conform to the MUTCD. Nonconforming signs are unlawful traffic control devices.

Texas

- Texas Transportation Code § 544.001

Requires the Texas Transportation Commission to adopt a manual for a uniform system of traffic control devices consistent with state law and, to the extent practicable, in conformance with the national system.

- Texas MUTCD (TMUTCD), adopted by TxDOT

The TMUTCD is the controlling manual for all traffic control devices in Texas and is adopted in substantial conformance with the Federal MUTCD.

Effect: Parking signs are regulatory traffic control devices governed by the TMUTCD. There is no parking exemption.

New York

- New York Vehicle and Traffic Law § 1680

Adopts the National MUTCD as the New York State Manual and Specifications for a Uniform System of Traffic Control Devices, except where state law provides otherwise.

- Prohibits state or local authorities from installing or maintaining any traffic control device unless it conforms to the adopted manual.

Effect: Parking enforcement based on non-conforming signage is unlawful under New York law.

California

- California Vehicle Code §§ 21400–21401

Authorizes Caltrans to adopt a state manual for traffic control devices and requires traffic control devices to conform to those standards.

- California Manual on Uniform Traffic Control Devices (CAMUTCD)

Adopted by Caltrans and required to be in substantial conformance with the Federal MUTCD.

Effect: Parking signs are regulatory signs governed by the CAMUTCD and must meet MUTCD standards to be enforceable.

Unified Legal Takeaway

Florida, Texas, New York, and California and every other US state and territory have all either adopted the MUTCD or their own compliant state MUTCD by statute or regulation. That adoption applies to parking enforcement because parking signs are regulatory traffic control devices. A non-conforming parking sign is not a lawful traffic control device and cannot support a valid citation.

Appendix C

Relevant MUTCD Regulations Governing Parking, Enforcement, and Informational Signs

I. Foundational Authority (MUTCD Part 1)

MUTCD §1A.01 establishes the Manual on Uniform Traffic Control Devices as the national standard for all traffic control devices on streets and highways open to public travel, including parking signs.

MUTCD §1A.02 sets the core principles of traffic control devices. Devices must fulfill a need, command attention, convey a clear and simple meaning, and provide adequate time for response. Ambiguous or cluttered parking signage fails this standard.

MUTCD §1A.03 requires uniformity in design, color, shape, and placement. Non-standard signs undermine enforceability.

MUTCD §1A.08 limits authority for placement of regulatory signs to public authorities or entities acting under their explicit authorization.

MUTCD §1A.13 defines traffic control devices broadly to include signs, signals, and markings that regulate, warn, or guide traffic, including parking restrictions.

II. Regulatory Parking Signs (Part 2, Chapter 2B)

Regulatory signs create enforceable legal obligations. Parking enforcement depends on compliance with these provisions.

R7 Series – Parking, Standing, and Stopping Signs:

R7-1 No Parking Any Time

R7-2 / R7-2a No Parking (Time Restricted)

R7-4 No Standing Any Time

R7-4a No Stopping Any Time

R7-5 Parking Permitted (Time Limit)

R7-6 Loading Zone

R7-8 Accessible Parking

R7-9 No Parking – Bike Lane

R7-20 / R7-21 Metered or Fee Parking

R7-201P Tow-Away Zone Plaque

R7-202P This Side of Sign

R7-203 Snow Emergency Parking Restriction

R8 Series – No Parking / No Stopping Variants:

R8-1 No Parking on Pavement

R8-3 / R8-3a No Parking on Bridge, Tracks, or Tunnel

R8-5 No Stopping on Pavement

R8-6 No Stopping Except on Shoulder

R8-7 Emergency Stopping Only

III. Auxiliary Signs and Plaques (Chapter 2B)

Auxiliary plaques are mandatory where conditions apply. These include:

Time-of-day restrictions

Day-of-week restrictions

Arrow direction plaques

Distance plaques

Except permit or except loading plaques

Failure to include required plaques renders restrictions ambiguous and unenforceable.

IV. Informational Signs (Part 2, Chapter 2I)

Informational signs provide guidance only and do not create enforceable obligations.

Examples include:

Parking payment instructions

Pay-by-phone or app instructions

Zone numbers

QR codes or website notices

Informational signs may not replace, contradict, or obscure regulatory signs.

V. Guide Signs (Part 2, Chapter 2D)

Guide signs may indicate the location or direction of parking facilities but cannot authorize parking where regulatory signs prohibit it.

VI. Pavement Markings and Curb Markings (Part 3)

MUTCD §3A.05 governs curb markings. Yellow or white curb paint alone does not create enforceable parking restrictions without proper regulatory signage.

VII. Visibility and Maintenance Requirements

MUTCD §2A.07 requires regulatory signs to maintain minimum retroreflectivity for nighttime visibility.

MUTCD §2A.08 requires illumination where ambient lighting is insufficient. Obstructed, faded, or unlit signs undermine enforcement.

VIII. Prohibited Practices

The MUTCD does not allow:

Vendor-installed regulatory signs

App-only enforcement zones

Conflicting or stacked regulatory messages

QR codes as the sole notice of restriction

Private branding on regulatory signs

IX. Enforcement Rule

Parking enforcement is lawful only where restrictions are created by properly authorized, properly placed, MUTCD-compliant regulatory signs. Apps, meters, and vendors do not create legal authority.

Appendix D

App Proud "Success" Stories in Their Own Words

Vendor Success Equals Optimized Extraction from Your Wallet

Across the parking technology industry, vendors proudly publish "success stories" highlighting revenue increases, improved compliance, and enforcement efficiency. What these case studies share is a consistent definition of success: increased extraction from motorists with zero attention paid to fairness.

In many instances, these gains are achieved through systems built upon confusing, obscured, or noncompliant signage regimes. Vendors design, deploy, and promote enforcement technology that depends on motorists failing to receive clear, lawful notice—then celebrate the resulting fines and fees as operational victories.

The following are representative vendor-published success narratives, summarized with their own metrics and language. The common thread is that "success" is measured not by fewer violations or fairer systems, but by how effectively money is extracted from the public.

Vendor-Published Success Stories (Revenue / Compliance / Citations)

1. Adaptive Recognition—Grīziņdārzs Parking (Riga, Latvia)(The Park Grift goes Global)

Vendor: Adaptive Recognition

Outcome: Reported ~25% increase in parking revenue after implementation of automated ANPR systems that detect, bill, and enforce without barriers or onsite staff.

Success Metrics: Revenue growth, reduced staffing, automated enforcement. Source: Vendor case study. adaptiverecognition.com

2. ParkMobile—Pittsburgh "Go Mobile PGH" (Pittsburgh, PA)

Vendor/Platform: ParkMobile

Outcome: City reported substantially increased parking revenue attributed to mobile payment adoption and better compliance (vendor says revenue has "rocketed" since the app's deployment).

Reported Results: Since enabling mobile payments, parking revenue in Pittsburgh increased by $13 million over time vs. 2012.

Source: ParkMobile case collection. parkmobile.io

3. Passport—Multiple City Case Studies (e.g., Bend, Denver)

Vendor: Passport (Passport Inc.)

Outcomes Described: Cities like Bend, OR and Denver, CO using Passport-enabled curb management and enforcement infrastructure have improved compliance tracking and streamlined enforcement workflows (vendor framing).

Several Passport case studies emphasize better connected enforcement, digital payments, and permit flexibility as drivers of increased compliance and operational data quality.

Source: Passport case study archive. Passport

4. T2 Systems—Various Municipal & Campus Deployments

Vendor: T2 Systems Outcomes Documented in Customer Success Stories:

University of Utah and *University of Oklahoma* campuses reported improved efficiency, streamlined citation services, and in some cases boosted revenue recovery via centralized citation management.

Gettysburg Borough reported $1.5M+ in parking revenue after modernizing enforcement and permit processes.

Vendor Framing: Case studies and success pages list revenue optimization and better enforcement workflows as key benefits of adopting their platform.

Source: T2 Systems customer success resources.

5. Softjourn / Generic Parking App Development Success Template Technology:

Parking management and enforcement apps

Claimed Outcomes: *Revenue generation* from increased compliance and smart enforcement

Collection of overdue parking violations via digital platforms Decreased operating costs through automation

These benefits are commonly cited in vendor "parking app" development marketing and case sheets.

Source: Softjourn industry summary. Softjourn Inc.

6. St. Augustine: Passport Parking and Revenue Expansion

St. Augustine is prominently featured by Passport—often branded as "Passport Parking"—as a mobile parking success story. According to Passport's published materials, after the city implemented its mobile payment platform in 2019, St. Augustine experienced approximately an 84–85% increase in parking revenue through 2020, including during the COVID-19 pandemic. Passport attributes this growth to expanded mobile adoption, improved compliance, and the efficiency of contactless payment. The case is presented as evidence that digital parking ecosystems can enhance fiscal resilience during economic disruption.

From an operational standpoint, the Passport model emphasizes centralized management, real-time enforcement integration, and reduced reliance on physical infrastructure. Mobile platforms eliminate cash handling, reduce kiosk maintenance, and streamline citation processing. During the pandemic, contactless payment was framed as both a safety measure and an efficiency upgrade. Municipalities facing budget volatility were drawn to systems promising scalable, technology-driven revenue capture.

The revenue increase, however, reflects more than convenience alone. Mobile platforms can increase compliance through automated reminders, extended enforcement windows, simplified citation issuance, and integrated time tracking. As kiosks are reduced and app usage becomes dominant, the system becomes more enforceable and more measurable. In that environment, revenue growth may signal structural optimization rather than merely increased demand.

The St. Augustine example illustrates the broader policy debate. Passport presents the data point as modernization and performance improvement. Critics question whether the system is calibrated primarily for efficiency or for extraction. The numbers are undisputed; the implications remain contested.

Notes on These "Success Stories"

What the vendors emphasize in these stories:

Revenue growth (more meters paid, more fines collected)

Improved compliance measures via automated detection or mobile payment

Reduced manual overhead / faster enforcement workflows

Across deployments, even internationally, success is measured by how effectively violations are detected, processed, and paid—not whether the underlying rules were clearly communicated or lawfully posted or fair.

In each of these cases, vendors define success through dashboards, collection rates, and revenue growth. What is omitted is equally telling: whether motorists received lawful notice, whether signage complied with governing standards, or whether violations declined because rules were understood.

Instead, the industry celebrates systems that convert confusion into cash—and congratulates itself for the efficiency of the extraction.

Appendix E

Florida Attorney General Complaint

COMPLAINT TO THE FLORIDA ATTORNEY GENERAL

Consumer Protection · Unfair & Deceptive Trade Practices · Minors · Privacy

To:

Office of the Florida Attorney General

Consumer Protection Division

State of Florida

Dated:

I. COMPLAINANT

National Association of American Defrauded Parkers (NAADP): A consumer-advocacy organization representing tens of thousands of motorists affected by unlawful parking enforcement practices, coercive mobile-application systems, and improper data collection throughout the State of Florida.

II. AUTHORIZED REPRESENTATIVE

Kerry Lutz

Founder & Managing Director, NAADP

Email: khl@kerrylutz.com

This complaint is submitted in a representative capacity and in the public interest.

III. OVERVIEW AND BASIS OF COMPLAINT

This complaint requests investigation and enforcement action against multiple Florida municipalities and private parking-application companies engaged in a coordinated system of unfair, deceptive, and unlawful parking enforcement practices.

These practices include issuing parking citations based on non-compliant or absent regulatory signage, coercing motorists into private digital contracts as a condition of lawful parking, collecting and monetizing personal and geolocation data without meaningful consent, and unlawfully contracting with minors.

Upon information and belief, these practices are widespread and prevalent throughout the State of Florida and reflect a standardized enforcement and revenue model rather than isolated incidents.

IV. UNLAWFUL PARKING ENFORCEMENT BASED ON NON-COMPLIANT SIGNAGE

Florida has adopted the Manual on Uniform Traffic Control Devices (MUTCD), which mandates that parking restrictions—being regulatory in nature—must be communicated by compliant R-series regulatory signs.

Parking meters and mobile applications are not traffic control devices and cannot lawfully create, modify, or replace parking regulations. Nevertheless, municipalities across Florida issue parking citations and demand payment in areas where no MUTCD-compliant signage exists or where signage is improperly placed, improperly colored, non-reflective, obscured, or otherwise non-compliant.

As a result, motorists are cited for violations of parking restrictions that are not lawfully established or posted.

V. MUTCD NON-COMPLIANCE AS AN UNFAIR AND DECEPTIVE TRADE PRACTICE

Issuing parking citations and collecting revenue based on non-existent or unlawfully posted parking regulations constitutes an unfair and deceptive act or practice under the Florida Deceptive and Unfair Trade Practices Act (FDUTPA).

Consumers are misled into believing lawful restrictions exist, enforcement relies on constructive notice that the MUTCD does not permit, and the illegality of the underlying restriction is never disclosed. This results in the collection of money under false pretenses.

VI. COERCED CONTRACTING AND UNLAWFUL CONTRACTING

A. Coerced Contracting of Adults

Motorists are coerced into digital contracts because payment is demanded under threat of citation, fines, towing, or escalation, there is no meaningful non-digital alternative, and no opportunity to review contractual terms at the curb. Contracts entered under such conditions are coercive and not consensual.

B. Unlawful Contracting with Minors

Minors lack legal capacity to enter binding contracts under Florida law. Nevertheless, parking systems require minors to accept terms of service, waive privacy rights, and authorize geolocation tracking without age verification, parental consent, or parental notification. Each such transaction constitutes a void contract and unlawful data transfer.

VII. PRIVACY AND DATA-SHARING VIOLATIONS

Parking application vendors collect precise location and personal data and share such data with numerous third parties. These practices are buried in dense digital terms, impossible to review at the point of enforcement, and coerced through threat of citation. The conduct is particularly egregious where minors' data is involved and constitutes an independent violation of Florida's Digital and Data Privacy protections.

VIII. VIOLATIONS OF FLORIDA'S DIGITAL / DATA PRIVACY BILL OF RIGHTS

Florida has enacted comprehensive digital and data-privacy protections governing the collection, processing, and sharing of personal data, including heightened protections for sensitive data and the personal data of minors.

The parking-enforcement and payment systems described herein violate these protections by conditioning lawful parking on mandatory acceptance of digital terms, coercing "consent" under threat of citation, fines, towing, or escalation, and collecting precise geolocation and personal data without freely given, informed, and revocable consent.

These violations are particularly egregious with respect to minors. Parking application systems routinely require minors to accept terms of service, authorize continuous geolocation tracking, and permit data sharing with third parties without age verification, parental consent, or parental notice. Such practices constitute unlawful data collection and transfer and are prohibited under Florida law.

Consent obtained through coercion, lack of meaningful alternatives, or inability to review terms at the point of enforcement is legally invalid. Municipal adoption of app-dependent parking enforcement systems therefore results in systematic violations of Florida's Digital and Data Privacy Bill of Rights and exposes both vendors and participating municipalities to enforcement action, civil penalties, and injunctive relief.

IX. MUNICIPAL PARTICIPATION AND BENEFIT

Municipalities actively participate by adopting app-dependent enforcement regimes, delegating enforcement authority to private vendors, and receiving revenue from app-mediated payments and citations, creating a public-private enforcement system that externalizes legal and privacy risk onto consumers.

X. STATEWIDE SCOPE

Upon information and belief, substantially similar practices are widespread, prevalent, and systemic throughout the State of Florida, affecting numerous municipalities and consumers daily. Statewide investigation and relief are therefore warranted.

XI. RELIEF REQUESTED

The National Association of American Defrauded Parkers respectfully requests that the Florida Attorney General open a statewide investigation; examine MUTCD compliance; investigate coerced and void contracting practices; investigate data-collection and sharing practices; require age gating, parental consent, and parental notification; prohibit unlawful app-conditioned enforcement systems; seek injunctive relief, restitution, and civil penalties; and issue public guidance to municipalities.

XII. SUPPORTING MATERIALS

Federal complaint and exhibits, photographic documentation, parking-application terms of service, and data-sharing disclosures are attached or incorporated by reference.

CERTIFICATION

I certify that this complaint is submitted in good faith and is supported by documentary evidence and publicly verifiable information.

Submitted this 29th day of January, 2026.

Kerry Lutz

Founder & Managing Director

National Association of American Defrauded Parkers (NAADP)

Appendix F

Complaint To the Federal Trade Commission

Section 5 of the Federal Trade Commission Act – Unfair or Deceptive Acts or Practices

Unlawful Monetary Extraction · Non-Compliant Signage · Digital Coercion · Privacy · Minors

I. COMPLAINANT

National Association of American Defrauded Parkers (NAADP), A consumer-advocacy organization representing tens of thousands of motorists nationwide affected by unlawful parking enforcement practices, coercive digital payment systems, and improper collection and monetization of personal and geolocation data.

II. AUTHORIZED REPRESENTATIVE

Kerry Lutz

Founder & Managing Director, NAADP

Email: khl@kerrylutz.com

This complaint is submitted in a representative capacity and in the public interest.

III. RESPONDENTS

This complaint concerns private parking-application vendors, including but not limited to mobile parking payment, enforcement, citation, booting, and towing platforms, and their municipal partners that jointly deploy app-conditioned parking enforcement systems.

The conduct described herein reflects standardized, industry-wide practices rather than isolated or accidental misconduct.

IV. EXECUTIVE SUMMARY OF UNLAWFUL CONDUCT

Respondents operate a coordinated public-private system that extracts parking fees, citations, penalties, boot fees, tow charges, and related revenues from consumers without lawful authority, while simultaneously coercing consumers into invasive digital contracts and data-collection regimes.

Municipalities impose parking restrictions that are not lawfully established or posted because required regulatory signage does not comply with the Manual on Uniform Traffic Control Devices (MUTCD), as adopted by the states. Despite the absence of lawful restrictions, Respondents demand payment and impose penalties. Consumers are coerced under threat of enforcement into surrendering personal and precise geolocation data.

These practices constitute unfair and deceptive acts or practices in violation of Section 5(a) of the FTC Act.

V. FACTUAL ALLEGATIONS—NON-COMPLIANT SIGNAGE AND UNLAWFUL EXTRACTION

Parking restrictions are regulatory in nature and must be communicated through MUTCD-compliant regulatory signage. Across jurisdictions, municipalities routinely enforce parking restrictions where signage is absent, improperly placed, improperly colored, non-reflective, obscured, contradictory, or otherwise non-compliant.

Where required regulatory signage is non-compliant, no lawful parking restriction exists. Any downstream extraction of money—including meter fees, app payments, citations, late fees, boot fees, or tow charges—lacks legal authority and constitutes unlawful monetary extraction.

VI. DECEPTIVE SUBSTITUTION OF APPS AND METERS FOR LAWFUL NOTICE

Respondents falsely convey that parking meters, QR codes, or mobile applications create enforceable parking restrictions or substitute for lawful regulatory signage. Parking meters and mobile applications are not traffic control devices and cannot create, modify, or replace parking regulations. Representing otherwise materially misleads consumers.

VII. COERCED DIGITAL CONTRACTING AND DARK PATTERNS

Consumers are required to accept non-negotiable digital terms and privacy policies under threat of citation, towing, or escalation. There is no meaningful non-digital alternative and no opportunity to review terms at the point of enforcement. Respondents employ dark-pattern practices by burying material terms, obscuring appeal rights, and misrepresenting lawful obligations.

VIII. UNLAWFUL DATA COLLECTION AND SHARING

Parking-application vendors collect precise geolocation data and personal identifiers and share such data with third parties for analytics, marketing, and other secondary purposes unrelated to parking enforcement. These practices are inadequately disclosed, unavoidable in practice, and coerced.

IX. UNLAWFUL DATA PRACTICES INVOLVING MINORS

Minors routinely use parking systems to comply with posted parking requirements. Respondents nevertheless require minors to accept terms of service, collect and process minors' precise geolocation data, and share such data with third parties without age verification, parental consent, or parental notice. Each such transaction constitutes an unfair practice.

X. SECTION 5 VIOLATIONS—UNFAIR AND DECEPTIVE ACTS OR PRACTICES

Respondents violate Section 5(a) of the FTC Act by misrepresenting that parking restrictions are lawfully established when they are not; demanding payment where no valid restriction exists; coercing consumers into digital contracts; and engaging in unfair data collection practices. The conduct causes substantial consumer injury, is not reasonably avoidable, and is not outweighed by countervailing benefits.

XI. MUNICIPAL-PRIVATE COORDINATION

Municipalities actively participate by adopting app-dependent enforcement regimes, delegating enforcement authority to private vendors, and sharing in revenues derived from unlawful extraction, amplifying consumer harm while diffusing accountability.

XII. INDUSTRY-WIDE AND NATIONAL SCOPE

Upon information and belief, substantially similar practices are widespread across the United States. The challenged conduct reflects an industry-standard business model warranting nationwide investigation and relief.

XIII. RELIEF REQUESTED

The Complainant respectfully requests that the FTC open a formal investigation; prohibit enforcement based on non-compliant signage; prohibit app-conditioned parking enforcement; require lawful signage compliance and meaningful non-digital alternatives; investigate unlawful data practices involving minors; seek injunctive relief, restitution, disgorgement, and civil penalties; and issue industry-wide guidance.

XIV. CERTIFICATION

I certify that this complaint is submitted in good faith and is supported by documentary evidence and publicly verifiable information.

Submitted this ____ day of __________, 2026.

Kerry Lutz
Founder & Managing Director
National Association of American Defrauded Parkers (NAADP)

Appendix G

Complaint to The U.S. Securities and Exchange Commission

Municipal Securities · Material Misstatements · Disclosure Failures

To:

Office of Municipal Securities
Division of Enforcement
U.S. Securities and Exchange Commission

Date: January 29, 2026

I. COMPLAINANT

National Association of American Defrauded Parkers (NAADP): A consumer-advocacy organization representing motorists and stakeholders affected by unlawful parking enforcement practices and related financial misrepresentations nationwide.

Authorized Representative:

Kerry Lutz
Founder & Managing Director, NAADP
Email: khl@kerrylutz.com

II. OVERVIEW AND BASIS OF COMPLAINT

This complaint requests investigation and enforcement action concerning municipal bonds and related securities whose repayment is directly or indirectly tied to parking-derived revenue, including ticket fines, app-based payments, booting fees, towing fees, and administrative penalties.

Upon information and belief, municipalities across the United States have issued bonds backed by parking revenue streams that are legally defective, materially overstated, or unlawfully collected, without adequate disclosure to investors.

III. MUTCD NON-COMPLIANCE AS A MATERIAL RISK

Municipal parking enforcement nationwide is governed by the Manual on Uniform Traffic Control Devices (MUTCD), the federally recognized standard adopted by all states.

Parking restrictions are regulatory in nature and must be communicated by compliant signage. Parking meters and mobile applications are not traffic control devices and cannot substitute for legal parking rules. Despite this, citations are routinely issued where required MUTCD-compliant signage is absent or non-compliant.

IV. ILLEGAL PARKING REVENUE STREAMS SUPPORTING MUNICIPAL BONDS

Parking revenue supporting municipal bonds frequently includes ticket revenue based on non-compliant signage, booting revenue imposed without lawful predicates, towing revenue triggered by invalid citations, and app-based payments collected under unlawful enforcement regimes. Such revenue is unstable and subject to mass invalidation.

V. COERCED AND VOID CONTRACTING AS UNDISCLOSED RISK

Parking revenue is increasingly collected through private mobile applications requiring users to accept terms of service, privacy waivers, and arbitration clauses.

Adults are coerced into these contracts under threat of citation or towing, while minors lack legal capacity to contract. Nevertheless, minors are required to accept these terms without age verification or parental consent, rendering such contracts void and revenue legally contestable.

VI. PRIVACY, DATA, AND LITIGATION RISK

Parking applications collect and monetize precise location and personal data, share data with numerous third parties, and create significant regulatory and litigation risk. Any disruption to app-based enforcement directly impairs revenue streams backing municipal bonds.

VII. FAILURE OF MATERIAL DISCLOSURE

Municipal bond offering documents generally fail to disclose dependence on compliant signage, risk of mass citation invalidation, exposure from coerced and void contracts, minors' data risks, and regulatory enforcement exposure. These omissions are material to investors.

VIII. NATIONAL SCOPE

Upon information and belief, these practices are widespread and prevalent nationwide, affecting municipal issuers, underwriters, rating agencies, and investors.

IX. REQUESTED ACTION

NAADP respectfully requests that the SEC investigate municipal bond disclosures tied to parking-derived revenue, assess material misstatements and omissions, examine the legality of underlying revenue streams, require corrective disclosures, evaluate underwriter and issuer due diligence failures, and take enforcement action where appropriate.

X. SUPPORTING MATERIALS

Federal complaint and exhibits, state AG complaint, photographic documentation, parking-app terms of service, and data-sharing disclosures are attached or incorporated by reference.

CERTIFICATION

I certify that this complaint is submitted in good faith and is supported by documentary evidence and publicly verifiable information.

Submitted this ___ day of ________, 2026.

Kerry Lutz

Founder & Managing Director

National Association of American Defrauded Parkers (NAADP)

Appendix H

Notice of Non-Compliance and Demand for Removal

(Parking Enforcement & Payment Applications)

To Whom It May Concern:

This notice concerns a class of mobile applications used for municipal and private parking enforcement and payment. These applications are distributed through digital application marketplaces and are made available to the general public, including minors.

Based on documented practices, contractual terms, and real-world enforcement conditions, the undersigned asserts that the applications listed below violate fundamental principles of contract law, consumer protection, and data privacy, and are therefore unfit for continued distribution.

I. IDENTIFIED APPLICATIONS (NON-EXHAUSTIVE LIST)

The following parking enforcement and payment applications are representative of the affected category:

- ParkMobile
- PayByPhone
- Passport Parking
- Flowbird / Flowbird Parking
- ParkSmarter
- ParkChicago
- ParkWhiz
- HonkMobile
- WayToPark
- ParkNow
- ParkEV
- ParkBoston
- CityPark
- ParkDetroit
- MobileMeter
- PayStay

- EasyPark
- RingGo
- JustPark
- Parkopedia
- ParkRight
- ParkMe
- SpotHero
- Parking.com
- Park One

(This list is illustrative and not limited to the applications named above.)

II. COERCED MINOR CONTRACTING

These applications knowingly facilitate and enforce **contracts with minors**, despite minors lacking legal capacity to contract.

Key facts include:

- Parking occurs in public spaces routinely used by minors (schools, beaches, courthouses, downtown districts).
- Enforcement is immediate and punitive, including citations, escalating fines, vehicle immobilization (booting), and towing.
- Payment is required *before* a user can lawfully comply, leaving minors no practical alternative.
- Applications are presented as mandatory compliance mechanisms rather than optional services.

The use of coercive penalties to force app installation and payment constitutes **non-consensual contracting** and renders any purported agreement void ab initio when entered into by a minor.

III. FORCED WAIVER OF CONSTITUTIONAL AND STATUTORY RIGHTS

These applications uniformly require acceptance of terms that include:

- Waiver of the right to a jury trial
- Mandatory binding arbitration
- Class-action waiver
- Venue and choice-of-law restrictions

Such waivers are imposed as a condition of avoiding fines, towing, or immobilization, and are therefore:

- Non-voluntary

- Unconscionable
- Legally unenforceable as a matter of public policy

When imposed upon minors, these provisions are categorically void.

IV. PRIVACY AND DATA-SHARING VIOLATIONS

The applications require users to consent to extensive data collection and sharing, including but not limited to:

- Location tracking
- Device identifiers
- Payment and financial data
- Behavioral and usage analytics
- Third-party data sharing

Minors are incapable of granting informed consent to such practices. The continued collection and monetization of minor data under coercive circumstances constitutes a **privacy waiver obtained without capacity**, rendering it invalid.

V. ACTUAL KNOWLEDGE AND WILLFUL DISREGARD

Application providers have **actual or constructive knowledge** that:

- Minors are regularly subjected to enforcement zones requiring app use
- Municipal signage and enforcement practices leave no lawful alternative
- Enforcement personnel do not screen for age or capacity
- Payments are routinely extracted from users legally incapable of contracting

Despite this knowledge, the applications continue to operate without safeguards, parental consent mechanisms, or lawful alternatives.

VI. DEMAND FOR ACTION

Accordingly, the undersigned demands:

1. Immediate review of all parking enforcement and payment applications
2. Suspension or removal of applications facilitating coerced minor contracting
3. Prohibition on forced arbitration and rights waivers as a condition of parking compliance
4. Mandatory safeguards to prevent minor contracting and data collection
5. Disclosure of municipal and third-party data-sharing relationships

Failure to act exposes distribution platforms and application providers to ongoing legal, regulatory, and reputational risk.

Respectfully submitted,

Kerry Lutz
Consumer Advocate / Legal Author
America's Great Parking Scam: You've Been Robbed!?!

Exhibit I

Generic Public Records Request Served Upon Defendant Town/Cities

The following is a sample public records request that has been served upon every town and city that is a party to this action. They are required by law to furnish this information in a set time period. I look forward to sharing the results with you. All NAADP members will get early notification of any responses.

PUBLIC RECORDS REQUEST

To: Records Custodian

[City/Town Name]

[Department or Clerk's Office]

Pursuant to applicable state public records law, this is a request for the inspection and production of all records relating to the City/Town's parking enforcement systems, vendors, and associated mobile applications.

This request includes, but is not limited to, the following categories:

1. Contracts and Procurement

All requests for proposals (RFPs), invitations to bid, contracts, amendments, renewals, addenda, and exhibits relating to parking enforcement, parking payment systems, mobile parking applications, citation processing, booting, towing, or revenue sharing.

2. Communications and Negotiations

All emails, messages, memoranda, meeting notes, calendars, text messages, and other communications between the City/Town (including elected officials, employees, and consultants) and any parking app vendor, enforcement contractor, or related third party, including pre-award and post-award negotiations.

3. Travel, Entertainment, and Benefits

All records reflecting travel, meals, entertainment, conferences, gifts, sponsorships, or other items of value provided by or reimbursed by parking app vendors or enforcement contractors, including receipts, invoices, payee information, reimbursement requests, and approvals.

4. Legal Analysis and Risk Assessment

All legal opinions, memoranda, analyses, emails, or notes—whether internal or external—addressing:

• the contracting capacity of minors

• enforceability of arbitration clauses or jury-trial waivers

• data privacy and data-sharing obligations

• consumer protection or due-process concerns

• liability exposure related to parking enforcement practices

5. MUTCD and Signage Compliance

All studies, audits, reviews, legal opinions, or correspondence concerning compliance (or non-compliance) with the Manual on Uniform Traffic Control Devices (MUTCD), including the use, placement, color, hierarchy, or legality of parking signs and app-dependent signage.

6. Data Sharing and Monetization

All records identifying data collected through parking applications, how such data is used, shared, sold, or monetized, and any agreements governing such data practices.

7. Convenience and Credit Card Fees

All records, emails and discussions concerning the determination of credit card fees, convenience fees and app usage fees. Allocation of revenues to municipality and the service provider.

8. Quarterly and Annual Profit and Loss Statements and Financial Reports

All profit and loss statements for on-street parking since 2021, including but not limited to, parking fees, ticket fees and fines, towing revenue and booting fees. A list of every employee directly or indirectly employed by Parking Department or Authority, including their salaries, bonuses and any fringe benefits received as well as pension contributions on their behalf.

9. Summary of all Parking Revenue Bonds Issued

All parking revenue bonds issued, if any, including date of issuance, coupon rate, bonding rating and amounts issued.

This request covers records in any format (paper, electronic, text message, or otherwise) and applies to records in the possession of the City/Town or its agents.

Please preserve all responsive records. If any portion of this request is denied, identify the specific legal basis for each denial and produce all reasonably segregable portions.

I request a written response acknowledging receipt and stating the anticipated production timeline.

Respectfully,

Kerry Lutz

Author, America's Great Parking Scam: You've Been Robbed!?!

Open Letter to the Secretary of Transportation

Kerry Lutz, Esq.

Director

National Association of American Defrauded Parkers

Palm Beach Gardens, FL 33418

__________, 2026

The Honorable Sean P. Duffy
Secretary of Transportation
U.S. Department of Transportation
1200 New Jersey Avenue, SE
Washington, DC 20590

Re: Parking Enforcement, MUTCD Uniformity, and the Erosion of Due Process on America's Streets

Dear Secretary Duffy,

I write to you as a Florida resident, systems analyst, and author of America's Great Parking Scam: You've Been Robbed!?—and as someone who has spent the past year documenting a nationwide breakdown in on-street parking regulation that directly implicates the Department of Transportation's core mission: uniformity, safety, and public trust on our roadways.

Your early leadership at the Department—particularly your focus on operational accountability, modernization, and correcting long-ignored infrastructure failures—signals a welcome departure from bureaucratic drift. Parking enforcement is one such failure. It has quietly metastasized into a revenue-driven, vendor-captured subsystem operating outside the spirit—and often the letter—of federal traffic control standards.

Across municipalities nationwide, parking enforcement now relies on signage that fails MUTCD requirements for regulatory Traffic Control Devices, substitutes commercial app instructions for lawful regulation, uses non-standard colors and symbols, and requires smartphone access and private contractual acceptance as a condition of compliance. What drivers encounter is no longer regulation—it is coercive instruction, backed by fines, towing, and booting, but untethered from uniform federal standards.

If a regulatory rule cannot be understood without a smartphone, an app account, and acceptance of private contractual terms, it is no longer a Traffic Control Device. It is a paywall masquerading as law. The MUTCD exists to prevent exactly this outcome. Yet parking signage has become a loophole industry—one where municipalities and vendors alike behave as though compliance is optional or unenforced. The result is widespread non-uniform signage, enforcement without clear legal authority, growing due-process exposure for cities, and erosion of public trust.

This problem does not require new legislation. It requires clarity and enforcement. Specifically, DOT could reaffirm that parking regulations are regulatory traffic controls subject to MUTCD standards; clarify that payment instructions, apps, QR codes, and commercial branding are not Traffic Control Devices; require documented engineering judgment for parking sign approval; and issue guidance that non-compliant signage is unenforceable.

Parking enforcement is the most frequent and personal interaction many Americans have with transportation authority. When that interaction feels arbitrary or predatory, the legitimacy of the entire system suffers. Uniformity is not a technicality—it is the foundation of voluntary compliance.

Referenced exhibits are identified below and are available upon notice. In addition, a complete printed copy of ***America's Great Parking Scam: You've Been Robbed!?***—containing photographic evidence, statutory analysis, and public-record documentation—is enclosed for reference.

I would welcome the opportunity to provide full documentation and analysis. This is a discrete, solvable problem where decisive leadership would have an immediate nationwide impact.

Sincerely,

Kerry Lutz

Palm Beach Gardens, Florida

FOUNDATIONAL DOCUMENTS of Lawful Public Parking

Including:

- The Ten Commandments of Parking
- The Declaration of Parking Independence

A Record of First Principles, Notice, and Public Standards

The Parking Declaration of Independence and 10 Commandments

Restoring the Streets to the People Who Own Them

Preamble

When in the course of human events, a people discover that they have become nothing but dairy cows exploited to feed an illegal system—when their public streets are converted into private revenue engines, when their movements are harvested for data without consent, when contradictory signs, coercive apps, and algorithmic traps supplant the rule of law— it becomes not only their right, but their duty, to expose, confront, and dismantle the Parking Industrial Complex and the Parking Combine that perpetuate these injustices.

For too long, municipalities and their private partners have erected a labyrinth of unlawful signage, predatory digital gates, and opaque enforcement rituals designed not to promote safety, nor order but extraction. And for too long, the citizens have been told to simply pay, comply, and remain silent.

But a free people are not born to be milked. A free people are not born to be tracked. A free people are not born to be coerced by apps in order to exist in public spaces they already own.

Therefore, in the spirit of the Founders, and in defense of the public trust, we declare our intention to withdraw our consent from this system, to petition for redress of these digital and physical abuses, and to restore the curb, the street, and the public square to the people from whom they were quietly stolen.

Section I—A List of Parking Grievances

1. They have erected illegal, unreadable, contradictory, and non–MUTCD-compliant signage, designed not to convey clarity, but to confuse and extract.
2. They have compelled citizens to download private apps under threat of citation, creating a coerced digital gateway to public space.
3. They have concealed guest-payment options, misleading consumers in violation of disclosure laws.
4. They have harvested the data of minors without meaningful consent.
5. They have monetized real-time surveillance through license-plate tracking and predictive expiration algorithms.

6. They have entered into revenue-sharing agreements with private corporations.
7. They have denied due process with citations issued in zones lacking proper signage.
8. They have engineered deliberate opacity in the design of signage and rules.
9. They have exploited tourists and non-residents as institutionalized traps.
10. They have imposed disproportionate fines unrelated to civic purpose.
11. They have allowed enforcement before paid sessions expire.
12. They have ignored public petitions and complaints.
13. They have treated citizens as captive revenue sources.

Section II—The Rights of the Citizen Parker

1. The Right to Clear, Legal, MUTCD-Compliant Signage.
2. The Right to Pay Without Coercion.
3. The Right to Privacy.
4. The Right to Due Process.
5. The Right to Proportionate Penalties.
6. The Right to Algorithmic Transparency.
7. The Right to Public Ownership of Public Space.

Section III—Demand for Redress & Sunset of the Parking Combine

1. Immediate audit of all municipal signage.
2. Suspension of citations issued in non-compliant zones.
3. Mandatory display of non-app guest-payment options.
4. Federal investigation into data harvesting and COPPA violations.
5. Transparency in municipal–private parking contracts.
6. Moratorium on algorithmic expiration tracking.
7. Citizen-review boards for parking policies.
8. Sunset provisions on unlawful contracts.
9. Public hearings to dismantle Parking Combine influence.
10. Restoration of public trust through compliance and law.

Section IV—The Signature

We sign this declaration not in ink, but in principle. For the streets belong to the people.

And the people are taking them back.

The Tablets of Free Parking

As Revealed to Brother Elon (Musk) During His Pilgrimage to the DOT Temple of All That Moves

In those days when the curb groaned under the weight of unjust fines, and meter maids patrolled the land like vengeful desert nuns, there arose a seeker among the technologists —Brother Elon, son of Silicon, wanderer of tunnels and chaos theory. Desiring clarity—and perhaps a higher bandwidth of consciousness—he embarked upon a micro dosing pilgrimage to the DOT Temple of All That Moves, the sacred bureaucratic shrine where every stripe, signal, and sign is ordained in the great MUTCD.

Amid the incense of lithium vapors and the faint hum of a noncompliant HAWK beacon, a radiant cloud enveloped him. The STOP sign talisman glowed. His pupils dilated to a 1:7 aspect ratio. And the

MUTCD spoke.

Before him appeared two aluminum tablets, milled to federal thickness, laminated in retro-reflective sheeting, mounted with anti-vandal brackets straight from the holy procurement catalog. Upon these tablets were inscribed the Ten Commandments of Free Parking, shimmering with Type XI divine authority. And the cosmic voice—or perhaps just a rogue Traffic Engineer on mushrooms—declared: "Deliver these tablets unto the People. For the curb belongs to them, not to the Church of Latter-Day Enforcers, nor to the Apps of Extraction." Brother Elon staggered down the ADA-compliant temple ramp, tablets under one arm, yerba maté in the other, and proclaimed:

"Hear me, O Parked and Oppressed—these are the laws that shall restore your curbside freedom!"

And thus began The Parking Reformation.

The Ten Commandments of Free Parking

(Inscribed on the Tablets of Aluminum and Retroreflective Light)

I. THOU SHALT NOT REDEEM THE CURB FOR REVENUE

The curb is a public commons, not a municipal profit center.

II. THOU SHALT HAVE NO ILLEGAL SIGNS BEFORE THEE

All signage must obey the MUTCD—proper colors, fonts, arrows, and lawful placement.

III. THOU SHALT NOT TAKE THE STOP SIGN IN VAIN

No sign shall be mounted above it. Its talismanic purity shall remain intact for all generations.

IV. REMEMBER THE PARKING DAY, TO KEEP IT FAIR

For residents, workers, visitors, and the elderly, the rules shall be clear, simple, and free of entrapment.

V. HONOR THY DRIVER AND THY DWELLER

A city exists for people—not extractive enforcement.

VI. THOU SHALT NOT ISSUE FALSE CITATIONS

Where signs are illegal, missing, contradictory, or city-caused ambiguous, no ticket shall be written.

VII. THOU SHALT NOT STEAL WITH TOW TRUCK OR BOOT

Booting is not a sacrament; towing is not a tithe. These punishments shall fit the gravity of the offense—if any.

VIII. THOU SHALT NOT BEAR FALSE EVIDENCE IN APPEALS

Appeal systems must be real, impartial, and accessible—not rubbery, shadowy, or algorithmic denials.

IX. THOU SHALT NOT COVET THY NEIGHBOR'S CURB

Parking permits shall not be used as economic segregation or municipal caste system.

X. THOU SHALT NOT PLACE PROFITS ABOVE THE PEOPLE

No app, authority, consultant, or bond covenant may supersede the rights, dignity, and mobility of the citizen.

Photographic Evidence Section

Signage Conditions and Observed MUTCD Violations

The following pages contain photographic documentation of on-street parking signage and related conditions observed by the author in multiple jurisdictions. These photographs are presented as a factual visual record of signage placement, design, hierarchy, and messaging as encountered in the public right-of-way.

Each photograph is accompanied by one or more abbreviated legend codes identifying observed deviations from standards set forth in the Manual on Uniform Traffic Control Devices (MUTCD) and related regulatory guidance. The legend codes correspond to a standardized key provided at the beginning of this section. The use of abbreviated codes is intended to ensure consistency, clarity, and repeatability across multiple examples.

The photographs are presented without narrative commentary. The legend codes identify observable conditions only and are not dependent on inference, intent, or motive. Where multiple codes appear on a single photograph, each code reflects a distinct observed condition. In many instances there are additional violations, but for the sake of brevity, we only cover the major infractions.

This photographic section is intended to serve as a documentary record illustrating recurring patterns in parking signage practices, including the use of non-standard sign formats, app-based payment signage, improper sign hierarchy, and other conditions affecting clarity, uniformity, and enforceability.

All photographs were taken from publicly accessible locations. No alteration has been made to the content of the images other than cropping or formatting for publication. Dates, locations, and additional contextual details are available upon request.

Master Legend List (with Brief Explanations)

NON-TCD

Contains logos, branding, QR codes, or advertising.
→ Not a lawful Traffic Control Device.

LOGOS / ADS

Commercial or promotional content on a regulatory sign.
→ Disqualifies sign under MUTCD neutrality rules.

APP-AS-TCD

Payment/app sign designed or positioned to appear authoritative.
→ Non-TCD masquerading as a Traffic Control Device.

IMPROPER HIERARCHY

Payment or app sign replaces or visually dominates required regulatory (R-series) sign.
→ Payment instruction cannot substitute for lawful regulation.

IMPROPER COMBO

Regulatory sign mounted with non-regulatory or commercial sign on the same post.
→ Entire sign assembly is non-compliant.

NON-STD COLOR

Uses unauthorized colors for regulatory signage (e.g., blue service color).
→ Invalid regulatory legend.

APP-DEPENDENT

Requires phone/app to understand rules or comply.
→ Fails self-contained clarity requirement.

NON-STD ARROWS

Uses angled, decorative, or non-approved arrows.
→ Ambiguous curb regulation.

LOW MOUNT

Mounted below minimum height 7 feet or obstructed.
→ Unenforceable.

NO REFLECT

Lacks required retroreflectivity or is degraded.

→ Nighttime enforcement invalid.

CURB CONFLICT

Conflicts with curb or pavement markings.
→ Ambiguity resolved against enforcement.

INVALID PERMIT

Custom or non-R-series permit restriction.
→ Permit void.

Photos Taken in Different Cities (with violation legends)

Town of Palm Beach--(All photographs taken in the Town of Palm Beach, Florida, Home of President Donald J. Trump. Images show full sign assemblies including post, height, placement, and surrounding context.)

Observed condition: A blue ParkMobile payment sign mounted pretending to be an R7 Traffic Control Device.

Violations: APP-AS-TCD, IMPROPER HIERARCHY, NON-TCD, NON-STD COLOR, LOGOS/ADS, NO REFLECT

Observed condition: A blue ParkMobile payment sign mounted pretending to be an R7 Traffic Control Device.

Violations: APP-AS-TCD, IMPROPER HIERARCHY, NON-TCD, NON-STD COLOR, LOGOS/ADS, NO REFLECT

Town of Palm Beach:

Observed condition: A sign with arrows pointing downward to the ground, non-MUTCD standard.

Violations: APP-AS-TCD, IMPROPER HIERARCHY, NON-TCD, NON-STD COLOR, LOGOS/ADS, APP-DEPENDENT

Observed condition: A Green and white Resident Parking Permit sign complete with PB City Logo.

Violations: INVALID PERMIT, NON-TCD, LOGOS/ADS, IMPROPER COMBO, NON-STD COLOR

Town of Palm Beach:

Observed condition: App sign with arrows pointing to a yellow non-parking curb non-MUTCD standard.

Violations: APP-AS-TCD, IMPROPER HIERARCHY, NON-TCD, NON-STD COLOR, LOGOS/ADS, APP-DEPENDENT

Observed condition: A no parking, commercial loading zone with no arrows next to an app sign.

Violations: APP-AS-TCD, IMPROPER HIERARCHY, NON-TCD, NON-STD COLOR, LOGOS/ADS, IMPROPER COMBO, APP-DEPENDENT

Town of Palm Beach:

Observed condition: A valid TCD 30-minute parking sign displayed next to an App sign with logos and trademarks along with advertising.

Violations: IMPROPER HIERARCHY, APP-AS-TCD, NON-TCD, LOGOS/ADS, IMPROPER COMBO

Observed condition: A no permit only sign written in blue. Two additional smaller signs compact cars only and no backing into spaces.

Violations: NON-TCD, NON-STD COLOR, FALSEREG, NOAUTH MISLEAD

Town of Palm Beach:

Observed condition: Hybrid parking assembly combining a red regulatory sign with a blue, app-based payment sign on the same post. The app/payment panel visually dominates, uses non-standard regulatory coloring. Not recognized by the MUTCD (Worst sign observed)

Violations: APP-AS-TCD, IMPROPER HIERARCHY, NON-TCD, NON-STD COLOR, LOGOS/ADS, IMPROPER COMBO, APP-DEPENDENT

Observed condition: Mirror image of opposite sign. Posted to show sign is in regular use by Town of Palm Beach

Violations: APP-AS-TCD, IMPROPER HIERARCHY, NON-TCD, NON-STD COLOR, LOGOS/ADS, IMPROPER COMBO, APP-DEPENDENT

City of Boca Raton:

Observed condition: Stacked parking signs mounted near a storefront, combining metered parking instructions with a time-limit sign, parallel to street and not observable to oncoming traffic, creating ambiguous and cluttered parking control.

Violations: NON-TCD, IMPROPER ORIENTATION, VISIBILITY OBSTRUCTED, IMPROPER COMBO, IMPROPER HIERARCHY, NON-STD FORMAT

Observed condition: Stacked, non-standard parking signs mounted low and oriented parallel to the roadway near a commercial building, mixing parking instructions, arrows, and commercial branding, with visibility degraded at night and no clear MUTCD-compliant parking control device.

Violations: NON-TCD, LOGOS/ADS, IMPROPER COMBO, IMPROPER HIERARCHY, NON-STD FORMAT, NON-REFLECTIVE, IMPROPER HEIGHT, IMPROPER ORIENTATION, VISIBILITY OBSTRUCTED

City of Boca Raton:

Observed condition: App-based parking meter sign mounted parallel to the street, presenting itself as a traffic control device despite being app-directed, with commercial branding and non-standard colors, oriented so approaching drivers receive inadequate notice

Violations: APP-AS-TCD, NON- TCD, IMPROPER ORIENTATION, VISIBILITY OBSTRUCTED, LOGOS/ADS, NON-STD COLOR, IMPROPER COMBO, APP-DEPENDENT

Observed condition: Stacked parking signs mounted on a single post, combining metered parking instructions with app-based payment messaging and a time-limit sign, partially angled toward the roadway, resulting in reduced legibility for approaching drivers and unclear curbside notice.

Violations: APP-AS-TCD, NON-TCD, IMPROPER ORIENTATION, VISIBILITY OBSTRUCTED, IMPROPER COMBO, IMPROPER HIERARCHY, NON-STD FORMAT, APP-DEPENDENT

City of Riviera Beach (Singer Island), where it all started:

Observed condition: Low-mounted, pastel-colored parking sign placed directly in front of vehicle spaces, advertising private retail parking and app-based payment, positioned below typical sightlines and easily obscured by SUVs or trucks.

Violations: NON-TCD, LOGOS/ADS, NON-STD COLOR, NON-REFLECTIVE, IMPROPER HEIGHT, VISIBILITY OBSTRUCTED, APP-AS-TCD, APP-DEPENDENT

Observed condition: Low-mounted, pastel-colored sign stack in a park setting advertising private parking privileges, combined with a beach/walking promo sign, using logos and non-reflective materials, with no posted times or days of enforcement.

Violations: NON-TCD · LOGOS/ADS, NON-STD COLOR, NON-REFLECTIVE, IMPROPER HEIGHT, IMPROPER COMBO, MISSING TIMES/DAYS

City of West Palm Beach:

Observed condition: The following pictures were taken in the vicinity of the Paul G. Rogers Courthouse in Downtown West Palm Beach, which is where my action against the Town of Palm Beach, the Cities of Boca Raton, Riviera Beach, West Palm Beach, Delray Beach and Fort Lauderdale is being filed.

Observed condition: No parking signs present near the Rogers Courthouse. Without a Traffic Control Device, no regulation is lawfully conveyed. No notice, due process. Also violation of Americans with Disability Act.

Violations: No signage pursuant to MUTCD §1A.01 – Traffic control devices are required to convey official traffic regulations. No ADA-compliant signage is present identifying accessible parking spaces, accessible routes, or the location of ADA parking accommodations.

City of West Palm Beach:

Observed condition: No signs present, only attempted notice is a sticker with zone number and times of enforcement.

Violations: NON-TCD, APP-AS-TCD, IMPROPER HIERARCHY APP-DEPENDENT At a courthouse, the lack of ADA-compliant parking signage creates a standalone civil rights violation. ADA 42 U.S.C. § 12132 No qualified individual with a disability shall, by reason of such disability, be excluded from participation in or be denied the benefits of the services, programs, or activities of a public entity…

Observed condition: No signs present, only attempted notice is a sticker with zone number and times of enforcement. In an area away from courthouse.

Violations: NON-TCD · APP-AS-TCD · IMPROPER HIERARCHY · APP-DEPENDENT At a courthouse, the lack of ADA-compliant parking signage creates a standalone civil rights violation. ADA 42 U.S.C. § 12132 No qualified individual with a disability shall, by reason of such disability, be excluded from participation in or be denied the benefits of the services, programs, or activities of a public entity…

City of Delray Beach:

Observed condition: Multiple stacked, non-standard signs on a single post near a building entrance, mixing app-directed pickup/drop-off messaging with a non-recognized parking restriction and advisory signage, without a clear MUTCD parking control device.

Violations: NON-TCD, IMPROPER COMBO, IMPROPER HIERARCHY, NON-STD COLOR, NO SUCH SIGNS UNDER MUTCD, LOW MOUNT

Observed condition: "Christmas tree" sign stack on a single pole combining a blue parking symbol, multi-line time/payment instructions, zone number placard, and separate app-based meter kiosk, creating cluttered, app-dependent parking control without a single clear MUTCD parking sign.

Violations: NON-TCD, APP-AS-TCD, IMPROPER COMBO, IMPROPER HIERARCHY, NON-STD FORMAT, APP-DEPENDENT, LOW MOUNT

City of Fort Lauderdale:

Observed condition: App-based parking sign mounted on a pole in front of a retail storefront, using commercial branding, QR-style payment instructions, and non-standard colors, presenting itself as a parking control device without MUTCD-recognized format or clear curbside regulatory notice.

Violations: APP-AS-TCD, NON-TCD, LOGOS/ADS, NON-STD COLOR, APP-DEPENDENT

Observed Condition: App-based parking sign mounted parallel to street, using commercial branding, QR-style payment instructions, and non-standard colors, presenting itself as a parking control device without MUTCD-recognized format or clear curbside regulatory notice.

Violations: PP-AS-TCD, NON-TCD, NON-STD COLOR, IMPROPER HEIGHT, VISIBILITY OBSTRUCTED, APP-DEPENDENT, IMPROPER ORIENTATION

City of Fort Lauderdale:

Observed condition: Back-to-back sign installation on a single pole combining a standard R7 NO PARKING / Tow-Away sign with a large, print and graphic-heavy "paybyphone" using non-standard colors, app store logos Fort Lauderdale Logo, credit card logos and layout, creating conflicting messaging, poor legibility, and unclear curbside regulation. Your eye has no idea where to go.

Violations: IMPROPER COMBO, IMPROPER HIERARCHY, NON-STD FORMAT, NON-STD COLOR, IMPROPER ORIENTATION, VISIBILITY OBSTRUCTED, APP Dependent, LOGOS/ADS, WRONG FONTS, TYPEFACE TOO SMALL FOR TIME

Observed condition: Side by side parking signs on a single pole combining a graphic-heavy parking schedule board with an app-based payment sign, using non-standard colors and formats, oriented inconsistently toward the street, resulting in cluttered, app-dependent parking control without clear MUTCD-recognized regulation.

Violations: APP-AS-TCD, NON-TCD, IMPROPER COMBO, IMPROPER HIERARCHY, NON-STD FORMAT, NON-STD COLOR, IMPROPER ORIENTATION, VISIBILITY OBSTRUCTED, APP-DEPENDENT

Made in the USA
Monee, IL
14 September 2026

62980080R00090